ADVICE FOR LIFE

A Woman's

Guide to AIDS

Risks and

Prevention

CHRIS NORWOOD

ADVICE FOR LIFE

Chris Norwood

ADVICE FOR LIFE

A Woman's Guide to Aids Risks and Prevention

A National Women's Health Network Guide

Pantheon Books
New York

All rights reserved under International and Pan-American Copyright Conventions. Published in the United States by Pantheon Books, a division of Random House, Inc., New York, and simultaneously in Canada by Random House of Canada Limited, Toronto.

Library of Congress Cataloging-in-Publication Data

Norwood, Chris.
Advice for life.
"A National Women's Health Network Guide."
Includes index.
1. AIDS (Disease)—Prevention. 2. Women—Health and hygiene. I. National Women's Health Network (U.S.) II. Title. [DNLM: 1. Acquired Immunodeficiency Syndrome—prevention & control —United States—popular works.
2. Women—popular works. WD 308 N894g]
RC607.A26N67   1987   362.1'969792   87-42540
ISBN 0-394-75428-X (pbk.)

DESIGNED BY QUINN HALL

Manufactured in the United States of America
FIRST EDITION

Contents

Aids, not AIDS

In our effort to understand AIDS, the acronym given to name the disease has turned out to be of little help. AIDS stands for Acquired Immune Deficiency Syndrome. Yet we suspect that the virus that causes AIDS may harm people without causing an immune deficiency, by attacking the brain directly, for example. Most misleading, AIDS is not a syndrome: it is caused by a virus, which makes it a disease.

To me, the worst aspect of the acronym is that all those capital letters, marching across every scientific report and news story, only reinforce our fear. Just in themselves, they seem to suggest that the disease is so big it is beyond our grasp and beyond logical efforts at control and prevention. Dr. John Seale, an English Aids specialist, strongly urges that, as a major step to managing this disease, it is time for a manageable name. "As the name Aids is now known to most people on earth," he writes, "it seems sensible to retain it as the name of the disease. However, the sooner the acronym AIDS is dropped, and it is spelled with lower-case letters as Aids, or aids, the better. The fact that the origin of the name was an acronym derived from *acquired immune deficiency syndrome* is now only of historical interest."

I totally agree. In this book I use the name Aids in the hope it will help the reader to concentrate on the subject without the constant intimidation to the eye—and mind—of a conglomeration of capital letters that are, in any case, incorrect. Many people may wish to do the same as their own small, but important, first step to taming Aids.

A c k n o w l e d g m e n t s

The generosity of the people in the "Aids community"—the scientists, counselors, doctors, nurses, and patients alike, who shared their time and knowledge with me—is staggering. But the first person I should thank is Mary Morgan, whose encouragement and tact restored my resolve when I was beginning to think this book would never be possible.

For their many contributions to my knowledge of Aids, I sincerely thank Dr. Robert Redfield and Dr. Donald Burke, the Walter Reed Army Institute for Research; Dr. Mathilde Krim, co-chair of the American Foundation for Aids Research; Dr. Judith Cohen, co-director of AWARE; Dr. Carol Harris, Bronx Municipal Hospital Center; the late Priscilla Diaz; Monnie Callan, Montefiore Medical Center; Lori Behrman, the New York City Gay Men's Health Crisis; Sunny Rumsey, the New York City Department of Health; Michael Shernoff, Chelsea Psychotherapy Associates; Dr. John Ward, the Centers for Disease Control; and Simone.

My extreme gratitude as well to Dr. Jeffrey Laurence,

director of the Aids laboratory at New York Hospital, for so graciously reviewing the manuscript.

For their important editorial contributions, I especially thank Sara Bershtel, Joel Honig, Andrea Eagan, and David Sternbach.

For support during this long siege or in general, I thank Louise Duncan, Arthur Prager, John Norwood, Jr., Frances Caldwell, Gordon Stewart, Ken Friedman, Tom Morgan, and, for her photography, Frances McLaughlin-Gill.

And, to end at the beginning, I thank Kitty Ross and Katherine Brown, the insightful editors at *Mademoiselle* who first suggested that I write on women and Aids. It is a real measure of the trouble we all have in confronting this disease that, even as a medical journalist, I at first thought I could not face the subject. I sincerely hope others won't be as slow as I once was; we don't have time anymore. To Kitty goes all the credit for insisting.

ADVICE FOR LIFE

Introduction

Women and Aids

"Can you imagine, if Aids hadn't been identified as a gay disease, what the outcry would be if even three women with a fatal sexually transmitted disease turned up anywhere in the country?"—Dr. Dean Echenberg, Director of Communicable Disease Control, the San Francisco Department of Health

When the history of Aids in the United States is finally written, it may be remembered above all that women were deceived. Science has never given us any reason to think that a virus—insensible and unknowing—would confine itself to predominantly male "risk groups." In Central Africa, equal numbers of men and women have been infected since the disease was first recognized there. That, in itself, was a severe warning. Even though Aids, in the West, first infected largely male populations of homosexuals, bisexuals, drug addicts, and hemophiliacs, it always was a sexually transmitted disease that could be expected to spread to women.

Yet, the fiction that Aids is not really a heterosexual disease has been maintained so forcefully in the United States that the federal Centers for Disease Control (CDC) did not establish "heterosexual contact" (sex between men and women) cases as an official risk category until 1984. By late 1986, the Department of Health of New York State—the state with the greatest number of female cases—still had not added "vaginal sex" to the official list of risk behaviors. By then, the virus that causes Aids had been in America since 1977, contrary to the idea that Aids is a new disease in the industrial world. As men in the original risk groups slept with women— often their wives—many of these women in turn began to get sick; totally unwarned, women had become the first victims of heterosexually transmitted Aids.

The year 1986 marked a crucial turning point. Until then, more than half of the American women diagnosed with Aids had contracted it through drug addiction. By sharing hypodermic needles with drug addicts who were unknowingly carrying the virus, these women had injected the Aids virus directly into their veins. In 1986, however, the cases acquired through sexual contact began to grow faster than cases caused by sharing needles. More and more women were sleeping with a man who had the disease or, more insidious, since the virus often does not cause symptoms for years after a person is infected, they were sleeping with a man who had the virus but did not know it himself. In many areas of the country, diagnosed sex-acquired Aids cases among women were increasing twice as fast as drug-acquired cases. By the spring of 1987, there had been 2,207 women diagnosed with Aids nationwide. Of these, 63 percent had died, compared with 57 percent of the 30,160 men with Aids.

Simply counting cases, however, is totally misleading. Like men, most infected women will probably not get noticeable symptoms for five years or even longer after exposure to the Aids-causing virus. For every diagnosed case, fifty to a hundred women may already have been infected with the virus. This means that results from testing women for viral infection, as distinct from waiting for diagnosed cases to emerge, give a much better idea of the spread of Aids and the number of cases that are incubating. Compared to men, very few women have been tested for infection; but the available figures suggest that some areas of the country are already in crisis, with the female infection rate rapidly approaching that of men.

The only large female populations that have been routinely screened to date are donors to blood banks and applicants to the Armed Services. Blood donors are largely middle-class, married, and over age twenty-five; and in most areas of the country they have an extremely low infection rate. This fact has been widely cited to reassure women—particularly middle-class women—that Aids has not yet reached the "general population." But many epidemiologists do not think we can make such easy conclusions from these blood donor figures. For example, among more than 300,000 donors tested from late 1985 to late 1986, the Red Cross of Minnesota did not uncover one infected woman. This encouraging fact loses significance when we remember that women who even suspect they may be at risk are no longer supposed to donate blood. But, certainly, there are infected middle-class women in Minnesota. "In our clinics," says Dr. Keith Henry, Medical Director of the Aids Unit for the St. Paul Department of Health, "we are starting to see a pretty steady number."

If, at second glance, the blood donor data are less than reassuring, the results of testing Armed Services applicants—a young, unmarried female population—are ominous. Nationally, only .6 per 1,000 women recruits are now infected with the Aids-causing virus, but in many areas the rate has reached 1 in 1,000. This latter figure is truly significant, as the history of the Aids epidemic shows. We now know that the infection rate of the gay community in San Francisco stood at 1 in 1,000 just before the major outbreak of cases there. Infection then multiplied very quickly—a trend that should greatly concern women. Indeed, in many areas of the country the infection rate for women recruits is already far greater than 1 in 1,000: in several counties and cities it has reached nearly 1 in 100. They include Brooklyn and the Bronx, New York; Essex County (Newark), New Jersey; Washington, D.C.; and San Francisco, California. Among afflicted areas, certainly Manhattan has to stand out as the worst example: there, by 1986, 1.8 percent of women—that is, one in fifty-six—who wanted to enter a branch of the Armed Services tested positive for infection with the Aids-causing virus. At that point, the virus is essentially out of control.

Unfortunately, the persistent image of the Army as a place for juvenile delinquents and minority groups has led many people to ignore even these figures. Contrary to popular perception, however, the Armed Services no longer accept anyone, male or female, who has been in jail or even on parole. Of the applicants, 77 percent are white, and all female applicants are high school graduates. "We are very concerned to find so much infection in this population," says Dr. Donald Burke, Chief of the Department of Virus Diseases at the Walter Reed Army Institute of Research in Washington, D.C. "Based on these numbers, I would predict a huge increase in female cases."

The point is that whatever the precise local rate of infection, there is no doubt that heterosexual women throughout the country are now poised to become *the fastest-growing* risk group. In 1986 the CDC estimated that 1.5 million people had already been infected with the virus that causes Aids. Some epidemiologists now believe that as many as 400,000 of them are women. From this perspective, the common projections of some 27,000 female cases by 1991 seem very optimistic.

What can be done? Absolutely, and above all, prevention counts. To a large degree, heterosexual women are the first developing risk group that has the advantage of being able to anticipate the virus's contagion. They are in a position to learn, to act, and to protect themselves and their loved ones. Testing, a major tool of prevention, was not widely available before 1985; and neither was the research showing that "barrier" contraceptives like condoms—and probably also foam and jelly—help block viral transmission. The issue is how to activate the will and commitment required for mass prevention.

At present, women who have begun to understand the urgency of prevention will not receive much help from public officials in combating or even understanding Aids. This is the lesson of New York, where women who acquired Aids heterosexually have actually been the city's fastest growing risk group since 1985, and it is a lesson that women throughout the country must learn. The astounding level of public denial that has accompanied New York's growing crisis is the first point. Even with 1,000 diagnosed female cases and a staggeringly high level of infection, the New York City Department of Health—despite considerable protest—still refused to add Aids to its official list of communicable diseases, a list that embraces other sexually transmitted diseases such as gonorrhea and syphilis as well as viral diseases such as mumps and measles. When a disease is on the list, the Commissioner of Health is required to make increased efforts at prevention and control. Meanwhile, the city's basic educational pamphlet, *Facts About Aids,* continued to claim blandly that only "a small number of women . . . have gotten AIDS."

Although New York is an extreme example, health officials throughout the country have had trouble talking directly and honestly to women about Aids. The reason is quite simple: admitting the huge increase in transmission from risk-group men to women means facing up to the harsh fact that

Aids is a disease that can threaten any and all sexually active people. By now, women have received three very contradictory messages about Aids: They *can't* get it sexually. They *can* get it sexually but only from mysterious risk-group men. But because, in the United States, not as many men have yet, in turn, gotten it from women, it's still not a *real* heterosexual disease that anyone should worry about.

These contradictory claims fly in the face of everything we know about sexually transmitted diseases. Every venereal disease has infected both heterosexual women and men. But, given the steady diet of misinformation directed at women, it is not surprising that even in an Aids-aware city like San Francisco, where the Health Department has talked frankly about heterosexual Aids since the epidemic began, women still seem to be reeling between denial and terror. In 1985, gonorrhea, the most immediately measurable sexual infection, actually rose by 6 percent among women in San Francisco, showing that sexually active women were still taking little care to avoid any disease. Yet AWARE, a San Francisco–based Aids education and testing program (the first in the United States just for women), had two counselors whose primary job was to reassure women who wouldn't believe they were healthy, even when a blood test showed they were not infected with the Aids virus.

Clearly, the primary task for women is to understand Aids, and the first step is to surmount the fear that is so paralyzing. "There's been a lot of resistance to educating women about Aids on the basis it will scare them," comments Denise Ribble, R.N., a health educator at the Community Health Project, an Aids outreach clinic in New York City. "I believe just the opposite. I believe that when women start to accept that they may have a risk, they empower themselves to start taking control and to protect themselves."

What should most rouse women to learn about Aids is

that self-protection is virtually impossible without basic and detailed information. The happy formula that so many health authorities have offered—just don't sleep with bisexuals or men who have used intravenous drugs—is not merely simplistic: it is dangerously simplistic. It completely ignores how deceptive (not to mention ludicrously naive) the quickly established risk-group categories for Aids really are. Plenty of men in the "homosexual and bisexual" category, for example, had only a few homosexual experiences, usually when they were teenagers. They may have acquired Aids then, but they could hardly be described as homosexual or bisexual. They are heterosexual, and current Aids education in the United States will do little to alert them—or the women they love—to the danger. Similarly, drug abusers are not all down-and-out street addicts. Some men who gave up drugs years ago have been infected, as have some who use intravenous drugs only occasionally.

The risk for women, moreover, can differ extraordinarily by geography, ethnic group, and life-style. Among diagnosed cases in New York City, most women who got the disease heterosexually acquired it from drug abusers. There, at least, black and Hispanic women have clearly been at greatest risk. In San Francisco, most diagnosed women who have sexually transmitted Aids got it from sleeping with bisexuals. However, Army studies suggest that women in other areas might be more threatened by promiscuous heterosexual men, those who are usually the first to get any "new" sexual disease. Of the first ten heterosexual, non–drug-abusing male Aids patients seen at the Walter Reed Army Hospital, for example, eight said they had slept with prostitutes or with fifty or more women in the previous five years.

Ironically, although Aids has been associated with promiscuity in men, among women it is wives and long-term girlfriends who have so far paid the highest price. Probably more than half the women now diagnosed with sexually transmitted Aids got it from their husbands or from men they had lived with for years. Over time, however, as Aids spreads into the unmarried population, this will change, as will the preponderance of black and Hispanic women among the diagnosed cases. In the Armed Services testing, for example, when the rate of female infection in an area reaches 1 percent (or more), it becomes almost equal for black and white women.

To understand the reality of risk, women must insist that state and local health officials make figures like these publicly available. "If you say all women are at equal risk, it's just not true, and it turns people off to say it," comments Dooley Worth, an Aids program developer for the Stuyvesant Polyclinic on New York's Lower East Side. "Still, when you try to pinpoint how women can know their risk, it's hard. The majority of women living with bisexual men, for example, probably don't know they're bisexual. And I don't think anyone knows how much intravenous drug use there really is in the middle class."

Even if they don't face an equal risk for Aids, then, all women have an equal stake in Aids prevention and policy. The slogans directed at women—"don't sleep with bisexuals or drug addicts" or, more recently, "always use a condom"— are not an adequate protection policy. Women need real education programs especially for them, in settings where they feel comfortable about asking very difficult, personal questions. How, for example, do you even ask a man to put on a condom? When should you or your partner get tested? Who will help you if you insist your husband be tested and he walks out? What should you do if you're pregnant and suddenly realize you may be at risk? How do you ask a man if he's ever had a homosexual encounter?

The current sloganeering health policy implies that women are solely responsible for their own protection. They are not. Combatting epidemics is a community obligation. Aids, as it spreads to women, is being treated differently from all previous sexual epidemics; none of the normal or ordinary public-health measures has been applied to its control. The Wassermann test, for example, first developed in 1910, was widely used to detect syphilis carriers and counsel them against spreading the disease, even though no cure was available at the time. In most states, those who come to a venereal disease clinic for any infection are now automatically tested for both gonorrhea and syphilis. But by the end of 1986, no state had routine testing for Aids infection. Obviously, it is essential that such testing be confidential. Without widespread testing, however, public-health officials have simply abandoned their responsibility to find and counsel men who, most of the time, do not realize that they are infected and capable of transmitting the disease to women.

Women everywhere will be profoundly affected by Aids. It will change their lives and their relationships with men. It will demand their attention and their sacrifice whether or not they have even the slightest risk of infection. As the traditional nurses of the sick, it is women who will largely end up taking care of a husband, son, or daughter who gets Aids. And as the protectors of family health, mothers will bear most of the responsibility for educating children about the disease. Substantial, factual information about Aids will be crucial for children who have reached their teens. Making their youngsters aware of this disease, without traumatizing them, will exact some of the deepest and most careful thought that parents can give. Simply trying to scare teenagers about sex has never worked, and Aids will demand more than sexual restraint: it will demand sexual wisdom.

The isolation of women in the face of Aids, a situation imposed on them by irresponsible public policies, and that they have accepted, must end. After a decade of women's activism, much of it focused on health, the silence of women themselves seems almost mysterious. The brief, frightening history of Aids has already shown the urgent need for concern and community activism. The task for women now is to determine how best to protect themselves from Aids, how to promote a constructive public policy of Aids education and prevention, and how to bring to this growing epidemic all the common sense and compassion that it is possible to summon.

Chapter One

The Virus at Work: Transmission and Symptoms

"The response of the U.S. Public Health Service to the spread of the deadliest virus to cause an epidemic among humans in the U.S.A. since the Service was founded, is, in effect, to say, 'Please don't bother us by reporting that people are being infected with the virus. Just let us know when some of them reach the terminal stages—and we shall then inform the public that this is the magnitude of the Aids epidemic.' "—Dr. John Seale, Royal Society of Medicine

The original myth that Aids wasn't a heterosexual disease has left women woefully confused about how the virus is actually transmitted during sexual intercourse. Basically, there is nothing mysterious about it. In the words of Dr. Robert Redfield, an infectious-disease specialist at the Walter Reed Army Institute of Research, Aids is "a plain, old-fashioned sexual disease spread by plain, old-fashioned vaginal intercourse."

In infected men, the virus is found in semen, the milky fluid ejaculated at orgasm. Semen is the vehicle that contains and carries sperm. Infected women carry the virus in the mucous lining of the vagina and in menstrual blood. Any of these body fluids—semen, vaginal discharge, or menstrual blood—can be a vehicle for the virus in sexual transmission.

People often have small skin breaks or bumps in the genital area, whether caused by venereal disease or just because everyone occasionally gets little genital nicks or bumps. The normal thrusting and friction of intercourse often creates or aggravates these skin breaks, which are so small they are known as microinjuries. Such injuries to the penis might never be noticed; an injury or tear of the vaginal lining is truly out of sight. Yet these tiny fissures are exactly what the virus needs in order to reach the various white blood cells that it preferentially attacks. Unlike red blood cells, white blood cells can circulate outside the bloodstream itself and are widely found in the soft tissues, including the soft underlayer of skin. They are the virus' main transport system, carrying it back to the capillaries and veins of the bloodstream, where it survives and multiplies.

Viruses are interesting microorganisms. They are not real cells or even technically "alive," since they can reproduce and multiply only by using the genetic material of a functioning cell. What has made the Aids-causing virus probably the most frightening virus ever known is that it is the first to attack the immune system directly. The immune system is the body's first line of defense against viruses and other disease agents. The particular cells, known as T-4 lymphocytes, that the virus targets, infects, and eventually kills are essential to regulating the immune response. As millions of them die, an infected person becomes increasingly vulnerable to infections and, sometimes, to certain cancers that the healthy body usually is able to fight off. Aids occurs when these "opportunistic" infections and malignancies finally appear, often years after the virus first entered the body.

Yet this virus fails to infect people through casual contact, such as sneezing, and coughing, or through sharing food, towels, or bathroom facilities. It cannot be picked up in pools or saunas, nor can it be transmitted through insect bites. To date there have been no diagnosed cases or infections traced to these causes. Simple observation reinforces the medical evidence. Children usually get most infectious diseases—yet relatively few children have Aids, and in the United States the only confirmed causes of disease in children are infected blood products and prenatal transmission from a virus-carrying mother. In Africa, a small number of children have also been infected by unsterilized needles used in medical procedures. If Aids could be spread by insects, coughs, or other casual transmission, not only would we expect to see thousands of cases among children but—in keeping with a common pattern for infectious diseases—children might well have more cases than adults.

There are three important reasons why the virus is not spread by casual transmission. First of all, the outer layer of skin on the face, arms, hands—indeed, all over the body—totally blocks the virus. Second, the small concentration of virus in sneezes and coughs isn't enough to cause infection by inhalation. Finally, except for sexual intercourse, the virus rarely appears to infect people even through a skin break. By now, hundreds of doctors and nurses who had open cuts have been sneezed or coughed on by Aids patients; hundreds of doctors and nurses have accidentally spilled contaminated blood and other body fluids from Aids patients on cut or bruised areas of their skin. But repeated and continuous testing in the United States, Europe, and Africa *has uncovered only three medical workers who became infected with the virus this way.* All three had severe skin lesions or cuts, such as scalpel wounds and acute eczema. And only three of the more than four hundred medical workers known to have stuck themselves with needles used on Aids patients have become infected.

Again, the difference may be that the virus isn't concentrated enough in sputum, saliva, or even blood spills to be very infectious or simply that the conditions of sexual intercourse help virus penetration—cuts or no cuts. After all, more than twenty-five disease-carrying microorganisms are transmitted mainly or exclusively through sexual intercourse. During sex, the virus is in a protected, moist environment, which is just what viruses prefer. The same reason that people like sex—because it is cozy—is why the Aids-causing virus does.

Most scientists believe that intercourse itself (penis inserted into the vagina) is the major route of heterosexual transmission. While other sexual practices are hard to evaluate separately, they are unlikely to transmit the virus. For example, although the virus is found in saliva, the amount is so small that kissing, including deep or "French" kissing, is very unlikely to be a means of transmission. Similarly, if an infected man performs oral sex (cunnilingus, licking the vagina) on a woman, it is very doubtful that the small amount of virus in his saliva could infect her.

While there was, at first, much concern that a woman who performed oral sex (fellatio, sucking the penis) on an infected man was at great risk of contracting the virus, there is now strong, direct evidence that this is not the case. Several studies have shown that the homosexuals who limit their sexual activity to oral sex, as many do, have not become infected. In some groups of homosexuals who have been studied for two years, not one uninfected man who had only had fellatio with his partners then became infected. Nonetheless, because of the high concentration of virus in semen, some scientists continue to worry about this practice. They advise women not to perform oral sex on an infected man—or, at least, not to take semen into their mouth—until there is more evidence.

For women, the major source of confusion has perhaps been anal (penis inserted into the rectum) intercourse, clearly the major form of transmission between homosexuals. Because scientists have so frequently proclaimed that the rectum tears so much more easily than the vagina during intercourse, many women have gotten the impression that as long as they have vaginal intercourse and avoid anal intercourse they are fairly safe. In fact, 90 percent of women with Aids interviewed in Africa, Europe, and the United States say they have never engaged in anal intercourse. Not surprisingly, many of them—including the infected elderly wives of transfusion patients—don't even know what interviewers are talking about when they ask the question.

The focus on anal intercourse has entirely confused the issue. Whether or not there is a special vulnerability associated with anal intercourse, this was not the cause of the rapid spread of Aids through the homosexual community. The cause was the number of sexual partners. "The significant factor is simple math," comments Dr. Redfield. "You had some homosexual chains where one person had a hundred sexual partners a year, and some of those partners had a hundred partners, and so on. The average number of lifetime partners of sexually active heterosexuals is now said to be twenty-three. Who knows how accurate that really is, but it's clearly enough to expect significant rates of infection, as we are seeing." In short, Aids travels by sexual intercourse, not sexual orientation.

The original doubts about heterosexual transmission become only more astounding with the knowledge that syphilis, the classic venereal infection, also needs to reach the bloodstream to cause disease and is often transported there by the same T-4 lymphocytes that transport the Aids-causing virus. Yet, syphilis is a much kinder infection, so to speak. It is highly contagious only for a few weeks after infection and then, during its second stage, for a year or two; and even when untreated it kills only 10 percent of its carriers. While we do not know how many infected people will ultimately get sick, the increase over time suggests that by ten years after infec-

tion more than 50 percent will have been diagnosed with
Aids. And Aids is always fatal.

This, then, is Aids, the terrible new—yet "plain, old-
fashioned"—disease. The final important question about
transmission is the efficiency, or rate, of passage from one
sexual partner to another. The major studies have consistently
shown that approximately half the wives or long-term sexual
partners of men with Aids become infected. At the Montefiore Medical Center, for example, 12 of 27 (44 percent)
wives tested positive for infection, and at the University of
Miami Medical School 10 of 24 (42 percent) wives tested by
mid-1986 were infected.

However, other studies have provoked considerable argument about the true rate of passage. The wives of hemophiliacs, to take one group, appear to have a much lower rate
of infection, as do the wives of men who were exposed to the
virus from transfusions. Infection rates reported in the Partner
Study at the University of California at Berkeley, for example,
are 46 percent for the wives of drug abusers, 16 percent for
the wives or girlfriends of bisexual men, a 15 percent rate for
the wives of transfusion-exposed men, and 10 percent for the
wives of hemophiliacs.

Two factors may help explain these differences. Some
scientists believe that the virus gets more contagious when
symptoms of disease develop. The studies showing a 40 percent or more infection rate are nearly all studies of the partners of *diagnosed* Aids patients, while studies showing a lower
rate include the wives and girlfriends of virus carriers who do
not yet have symptoms of illness. The longer a woman sleeps
with a sick man, in fact, the worse her own prospects. At the
Miami Aids Clinical Research Unit, of the women who continued to have unprotected sexual intercourse with their husbands for a year after they were diagnosed, 86 percent became
infected. (This happened largely because many of the Miami
patients do not speak English and did not fully understand the

danger or the need to use condoms. They now receive multiple counseling sessions.)

The frequency of exposure through intercourse also helps to determine transmission. Most partners of drug abusers in the Berkeley study, for example, were in long-term relationships, whereas many of the women who had slept with bisexuals had had shorter-term relationships (less than a year). Most men with transfusion-caused infection are over age fifty and recently survived serious surgery, circumstances that discourage frequent sexual encounters. And hemophilia may present a separate case entirely. Hemophiliac men do not seem to get Aids as often, or at least not as soon, as infected men in other risk groups. Possibly, their blood disorder interferes with the replication of the virus, somewhat protecting them from disease and their wives from its sexual transmission.

Even if, in a sad irony, the risk from long-term relationships is greater, women should not be fooled into thinking that a brief affair is perfectly safe. The first French woman to get Aids (now dead) almost certainly contracted it from a one-night stand in Haiti two and a half years earlier. One infected wife in the CDC transfusion group had intercourse with her husband only once after his surgery, and at least one woman diagnosed with Aids in San Francisco in 1986 had only one encounter with the man who infected her.

To sum up, a woman exposed to the virus through a steady sexual relationship for a year or more faces a 20 to 40 percent risk of infection, and as the man gets sick the risk may increase greatly. Though her risk from one-time exposure is small, it is certainly present. But these calculations are ultimately speculative, for we still have precious little research about transmission. In fact, only in Sweden have doctors actually traced a single "virus clump" as it passed through a succession of heterosexual partners.

That case began with a Swedish sailor we'll call Lars. He

evidently got the virus in 1979, after having slept with a prostitute in Haiti. On returning home, he had affairs with six women before getting married in 1983. The chain of infection came to light when a male sex partner of one of these women donated blood and tested positive. It is now the policy in Sweden to try to trace the sex partners of all infected blood donors, to test them, and to warn those who are carrying the virus against spreading it to anyone else. This tracing showed that three of the women with whom Lars had affairs, as well as his wife, were infected: a 57 percent rate of infection. The fate of these once healthy, hearty, white middle-class women is a strong warning to women in the United States and Europe: though the virus has taken longer to reach them, when it does arrive they can be just as vulnerable as women in Africa.

The vulnerability of men to infection from women is harder to evaluate. The very scant data on this subject in Europe and the United States suggest that heterosexual men may be less likely than women to acquire the virus from brief affairs but that, in steady relationships, the odds of transmission eventually even out. In short-term relationships, transmission from women to men seems to be less than 20 percent. The Walter Reed Army Institute of Research, for example, has traced ten male partners of a woman infected by a transfusion; only one was infected himself. The Swedes have traced seven male partners of the three women (aside from his wife) whom Lars infected; again, only one was a virus carrier. For very, very brief encounters we have the example of two Minnesota women who were members of sex clubs and were evidently infected by bisexual men; they did not pass on the virus to their more than twenty-five other male partners during the rather hurried circumstances of group sex.

Yet for the husbands or long-term partners of infected women, it is a far different story. Both husbands of two female transfusion patients seen at Walter Reed are infected. At the University of Miami, 3 out of 8 (38 percent) husbands of variously infected women have been positive, and 6 out of 11 (55 percent) of a male group of long-term partners being monitored at the Montefiore Medical Center in the Bronx are infected. These rates of transmission are virtually identical to those seen for male-to-female transmission in long-term relationships.

No matter what the relative efficiencies of male and female transmission prove to be, the need for full-fledged heterosexual prevention is evident and overwhelming. Certainly, there isn't a scrap of evidence that heterosexual men, as some health officials have proposed, are "uniquely resistant" to the Aids-causing virus. And, as we already know from experience with other venereal diseases, even when heterosexual men are somewhat less vulnerable to transmission, they still get a lot of disease. Men, for example, account for 60 percent of the gonorrhea cases diagnosed every year, even though women contract the disease more easily from one encounter. The point is simple: sleeping with more people spreads more disease. This is well known. What is not well known—or ignored—is that women *do* have to worry about contracting Aids from heterosexual men, as well as from those in risk groups.

Many women and men alike now spend endless time wondering if they are infected. At present, since there is so little routine testing, most people will find out only if they get symptoms. Knowing the symptoms is important to everyone's health and crucial to prevention. Knowing the symptoms can also help people from becoming obsessed with the fear that they have Aids when they don't. "The most important clue," stresses Dr. Carol Harris, Coordinator of Aids Activities at the Bronx Municipal Hospital Center, "is persistence. You can get the same early symptoms—weight loss, low-grade fever, swollen lymph nodes—for dozens of problems. With this disease, though, the symptoms don't go away."

The first thing to understand is that we still do not know whether infection inevitably leads to Aids. The virus that causes Aids, now internationally known as HIV (human immunodeficiency virus), is so new to concentrated research that it has barely received an accepted name; until 1986 it was known in the United States as HTLV-III, and in France it is still widely referred to as LAV. So far, in studies of homosexuals, only about 1 percent of men develop obvious symptoms within two years after HIV infection; but six years later, between 20 and 30 percent have diagnosed Aids. This research projects that 50 percent or more will have Aids within ten years after infection; but whether the same projection holds for women is not known.

The pattern of disease is also more complex and varying than was first perceived. Although "Aids" will undoubtedly always be used as the common name for any severe illness caused by HIV, we now recognize that HIV doesn't cause *only* Aids. As defined by the CDC, "real" Aids does not occur until an immune-deficient person develops certain opportunistic infections (the most common are *Pneumocystis carinii* pneumonia and the fungus infection, candidiasis) or certain cancers, primarily the rare malignancy, Kaposi's sarcoma. But HIV also causes a range of other illnesses—some severe, others relatively minor conditions that people can live with for years. And even with real Aids, there is no precise pattern. In most cases, the disease apparently develops slowly over years, but in some cases it develops quickly. Some patients get a number of early symptoms, such as swollen lymph nodes, severe fatigue, and persistent fever, before developing an infection; other patients don't. An opportunistic infection may set in before the patient has noticed any symptoms at all.

One of the first signs of infection that some people notice is a brief, flulike illness that may occur a few weeks to a few months after the virus invades the body. It is an indication that the body is "seroconverting"—massively producing antibodies to try to fight the virus. (After seroconversion the body usually has produced enough antibody for it to be detected in the blood test for HIV.) This illness, technically known as acute HIV infection, lasts from three to fourteen days and may include fever, sweating, headaches, and fatigue. The real clue, however, is that seroconversion illness typically causes a distinct rash, featuring little, scattered red areas on the front and/or back of the torso.

While this early illness has not been reported as often in the United States as in Australia and some European countries, it probably occurs most often when the virus is transmitted sexually. For instance, when they thought back, all four of the women infected by sleeping with Lars remembered such an illness; it had occurred from seventeen days to three months after the first sexual encounter, and all the women had had the distinctive rash, along with the other flulike symptoms. This first illness is the exception to the rule that HIV-caused symptoms are persistent; the rash, fever, and fatigue all go away. Moreover, seroconversion illness does not predict when or whether Aids will develop. Two of Lars's partners have now gone from four to six years with no other symptoms.

Another clue to infection may be discovered through routine blood testing. Pregnancy and various obstetric and gynecological surgical procedures make it necessary for younger women to have blood tests with some frequency. Whenever a routine test shows a deficiency of a blood element (cytopenia), particularly of white blood cells and platelets, a woman should consider having an HIV test. Normal results of a blood test in no way guarantee that she doesn't have HIV

infection; and, conversely, low counts of blood elements can
occur for any one of many reasons. But most infected women
apparently develop cytopenias before any noticeable symptoms, and infected women probably develop them faster than
infected men. "My advice for any sexually active woman with
a cytopenia would not be to discuss getting an HIV test but
to tell the doctor she wants one," says Dr. Craig Wright, Chief
of the Infectious Disease Clinic at Walter Reed Army Medical
Center. "And that goes for any man with a cytopenia, too."

A very obvious symptom and usually the first to be noticed, although it often doesn't appear for years after infection, is weight loss. Officially, weight loss becomes a possible
sign of HIV infection only when a woman has lost at least 10
percent of her body weight. "Again," says Dr. Harris, "the
major indicator is persistence. You keep losing weight, slowly
but steadily, for no apparent reason." Another early symptom, which may not surface for years, is generalized lymphadenopathy, or abnormal swelling of the lymph nodes.
They are "collection points" for the elaborate system that
carries away waste products produced by the body when it
fights infection; they are scattered throughout the head, neck,
upper arms, and trunk.

The easiest nodes to feel are located under the chin, behind the ears, in the back of the neck, and about an inch above
the middle of the collar bone. They feel like smooth, little peas
and are not movable like cysts. To count as enlarged they
must reach one centimeter (a little less than half an inch) in
diameter. To count as a symptom of HIV infection they must
persist for at least three months and in at least two sites of the
body, aside from the groin area. Enlarged nodes are so easy to
feel that generalized lymphadenopathy is often impossible
not to notice. "I have one under my arm the size of a grape,"
says one patient. The nodes sometimes feel tender and cause
discomfort or achiness.

Along with lymphadenopathy, or sometime later, many people develop a continuing fever (100 degrees or more) and night sweats. Again, persistence is the key; the fever has to last more than one month, and the night sweats are so severe that the bed linen will be drenched; typically your nightgown will be so soaked you can wring water out of it.

Before the disease was well understood, swollen lymph nodes and other early symptoms were referred to as ARC, or Aids-related complex. Now that we better understand the spectrum of the disease, the term ARC is passing from medical usage, and these symptoms are now said to represent "other HIV-associated disease." Even symptoms like weight loss, lymphadenopathy, fever, and night sweats are not signs that Aids is immediately on the horizon. About 70 percent of infected people with enlarged lymph nodes, for instance, still have not developed Aids after five years. "I leave them alone and they leave me alone," says Simone, a woman whose nodes have now been enlarged for two years.

If the HIV-infected person contracts one or more of twelve specific opportunistic infections,* she or he has Aids. These infections are called opportunistic because they are not usually life-threatening to people with a normal immune system. Although usually preceded by "milder" symptoms, opportunistic infections are sometimes the first problem to be noticed. The most common, often preceded by weeks of fever, night sweats, and a persistent, dry cough, is *Pneumocystis* pneumonia; it affects 64 percent of Aids patients. The second most common, affecting 9 percent of patients, is candidiasis, a fungus infection. To officially qualify as a symptom of Aids,

---

*The infections are *Pneumocystis carinii* pneumonia (PCP), chronic cryptosporidosis, toxoplasmosis, extraintestinal strongyloidiasis, isoporiasis, candidiasis (esophageal, bronchial, or pulmonary), cryptococcosis, histoplasmosis, mycobacterial infection with *Mycobacterium avium* complex or *M. kansasii,* cytomegalovirus infection (CMV), chronic mucocutaneous or disseminated herpes simplex virus infection, and progressive leukoencephalopathy.

candidiasis must infect the esophagus, bronchial tubes, or lungs. In truth, however, most infected people first notice candidiasis—or thrush, as it is commonly called—in the mouth, where it leaves very obvious white spots or a white coating on the tongue. Women are very familiar with genital candidiasis as the cause of frequent vaginal infections, sometimes referred to as monilia or just "yeast." While women with Aids sometimes do get severe vaginal infections, *vaginal candidiasis alone does not count as an Aids infection;* it is simply too common on its own to be considered a diagnostic indicator. Chronic herpes simplex is also an Aids-related infection. Herpes simplex is well known as the virus that causes cold sores. But be very clear that *a cold sore is not a sign of Aids.* HIV-associated herpes simplex erupts in large patches or severe lesions, on the face or other areas of the body, that will send almost anyone to the doctor.

The symptoms of several other Aids-associated infections often mimic each other. For instance, cryptococcosis (a systemic yeast infection), cytomegalovirus (a virus-caused infection), histoplasmosis (a parasite infection), and Aids-associated mycobacterial infections can all lead to either pneumonia or other severe respiratory illnesses. Cryptosporidiosis and isoporiasis, both parasite infections, cause severe diarrhea (five to fifteen bouts a day). Most of the time, however, because of the varying symptoms, even a doctor cannot diagnose the Aids infections without thorough testing. Obviously, anybody who feels as bad as these infections make a person feel belongs in a doctor's office or an emergency room. Something is seriously wrong, whether or not there is the least reason to think that HIV is the underlying cause.

The major cancer associated with Aids is Kaposi's sarcoma. Actually a malignancy of the blood vessels, it appears as dark purplish blotches (sometimes very small, other times very obvious) on the face, inside the mouth, and sometimes on the legs or feet, particularly on the soles of the feet. Because these blotches are flat, they are not easily confused with moles or other skin growths. For unknown reasons, Kaposi's sarcoma is seen primarily in homosexual men. It is not common in women infected heterosexually, although some 12 percent of women infected by drug abuse may get it. Lymphoma, a malignancy of the lymphoid tissue, in the two specific forms of non-Hodgkin's lymphoma and primary lymphoma of the brain, is the other official Aids-associated cancer.

In addition to the twelve opportunistic infections and two cancers now counted in the CDC definition of Aids, HIV infection can cause other severe illness, including tuberculosis and a growing list of other cancers. It can also lead to major and irreversible neurological damage, sometimes manifesting itself in erratic or bizarre behavior. "We're at the starting line when it comes to understanding the neurological disorders," says Dr. John Ward, an epidemiologist at the CDC in Atlanta. "What we don't know is how often they appear just as a result of HIV, without there being a further infection." The CDC is presently revising, and expects to almost continuously revise, the definition of Aids to embrace more diseases whose association with HIV is becoming clearer.

What we also don't know is the timing of the disease. As stated, in study populations of homosexual men, 1 percent develop symptoms during the first two years after infection, and 20 to 30 percent have diagnosed Aids within six years. However, women may get sick sooner. The Walter Reed Army Medical Center, for example, is now following more than 400 men and women from early infection through all stages of disease. Already, tests show that 60 percent of women, but only 33 percent of men, are immune-deficient, although they may not yet have noticeable symptoms. And women, once they have Aids, generally die sooner than men, perhaps because pregnancy increases the immune system's vulnerability to the virus' assault. Whereas some heterosexual men seen at the Montefiore Medical Center in the Bronx have lived for as long as three and a half years after diagnosis of an opportunistic infection, all the heterosexual women patients seen there have died within twenty-five months of diagnosis.

Even if it turns out that the disease progresses faster in women than in men, it will still take most women years to become even slightly ill. In one group of nine heterosexual women it took three and a half years on average from the last sexual encounter with the infected man before early symptoms were noticeable. And, among Lars's unlucky girlfriends, one has remained perfectly healthy since her bout of seroconversion illness in January 1981, and another has been well since she seroconverted in August 1982. Again, for women as for men, we simply do not know whether infection always leads to Aids or other HIV-associated diseases.

For women who are worried about symptoms, the major problem may be to get to a doctor to discuss the subject. Women who have a suspicious infection, as well as healthy women who are just worried, report again and again that doctors simply scoff at them for even raising the question. "But you, a woman—a *nice* woman—won't get Aids," is a typical response. Amazingly, even in New York City, Simone went for two years with enlarged lymph nodes, but not one doctor she consulted suggested that she have an HIV test. As recently as 1985, in the search for a cause, she had a biopsy for cancer. When her husband, who had given up intravenous drugs in 1979, developed Aids, her question was finally answered. "All that time," she recalls, "we were trying for a pregnancy. I can accept that my husband is dying. I can accept that I am infected. But if I had given Aids to my own child, I could never have accepted that."

Women have legitimate reasons to discuss Aids. Many confusing and largely—or exclusively—female conditions mimic early Aids symptoms: They include pelvic inflammatory disease (fever, abdominal pain, just "feeling bad"), emotional depression (often accompanied by unexplained weight loss), menstrual problems (night sweats, diarrhea), and anemia (overwhelming fatigue and sometimes aching bones).

At this point, any woman with the slightest suspicion of Aids should receive prompt medical attention. Immediate reassurance for those who are not sick is as important as immediate diagnosis for those who are.

C h a p t e r   T w o

Which Men Have Aids?

"What we've gotten with Aids is a lot of 'bean-counting' epidemiology, where you only recognize patients who fall into categories that epidemiologists have already decided exist."—Dr. Robert Redfield, Walter Reed Army Institute of Research

While the *how* of Aids transmission is obviously important to understanding both risks and prevention, understanding *who* is transmitting HIV is crucial for women. Unfortunately, the CDC method of categorizing diagnosed men into strict risk groups has made it appear that they are practically wearing neon signs. They aren't. No risk group is as simple or straightforward as it seems; the available studies offer only a rough portrait of the men most likely to be transmitters.

Moreover, risk groups do not tell us about people's real sex lives, and they are particularly deceptive about the prospects for heterosexual transmission. Health officials have too often cited these diagnosed cases and their risk-group categorizations to downplay the spreading epidemic; by emphasizing that only 113 of the diagnosed American-born male patients are "heterosexual contact" patients, they give the impression that only 113 heterosexual men in the country have been diagnosed. In fact, the majority of men in three other risk groups—drug addicts, hemophiliacs, and transfusion cases—are heterosexual; all bisexuals and a large number of homosexuals have slept with women; and many men categorized as having no known risk are thought to have acquired Aids heterosexually.

There is yet another problem. Although diagnosed cases remain a major source of information about the pattern of the disease, they do not reveal where the epidemic has arrived today. "When you look at the patients, you learn only who was being infected five years ago," emphasizes Dr. Mathilde Krim, co-chair of the American Foundation for Aids Research. Without substantial studies of the spread of infection, particularly among heterosexual men, women are left to regard Aids as not a "real" sexually transmitted disease. Let's look at the difference between what the diagnosed cases and current testing can tell us. In early 1985, for example, there were only two diagnosed male heterosexual cases in New York City; testing of a small group at Manhattan venereal disease clinics, however, showed that 10 out of 295 heterosexual non–drug-abusing men (3.4 percent) being treated for other venereal diseases were already infected with HIV. Even one such study immediately exposes the absurdity of the easy slogan "just don't sleep with bisexuals or drug addicts."

Understanding the shortcomings of risk-group categories is essential. These cases only provide rough guideposts along the epidemic's path. Especially for women, a major step toward prevention is to understand what public health officials really do—and don't—know when they are talking to you.

Of the six major CDC risk groups—hemophiliac/coagulation disorders, transfusion cases, drug addicts, homosexuals/bisexuals, heterosexual contact, and no known risk—hemophiliacs are both the smallest and best-defined group. By March 1987, there were 267 men with hemophilia or other coagulation disorders who had Aids, constituting 1 percent of all male Aids cases. Hemophilia, which occurs almost exclusively in men, is the most serious as well as the most common of the clotting, or bleeding, disorders. Untreated, hemophiliacs can bleed to death from minor injuries and bruises. Since the late 1960s, hemophiliacs have been treated by routine injections of clotting-factor concentrate, a process that permits them to lead quite normal lives. But because this concentrate is made from the pooled blood of hundreds of donors, hemophiliacs—there are twenty thousand in the United States—have ended up with an extraordinarily high rate of HIV infection. In the United States and most Western countries, between 80 and 90 percent of men with severe hemophilia are infected, as are between 30 and 40 percent of those with moderate hemophilia. For men with other bleeding disorders infection may be less but still significant. The Australians, for example, have reported that 25 percent of the patients with von Willebrand's disease, the second most common bleeding disorder, are infected.

At this point, hemophiliacs who have remained virus-free are almost certainly safe. They now have the double protection of a process for heat-treating the concentrate in order to kill HIV, first used in the United States in late 1984, and blood donor testing. They are also probably the risk group that has been most thoroughly counseled about sexual transmission. "Most of those we see now are either using condoms or being celibate. We tell them all to assume they're infected, whether they've had a test or not," says Dr. Natalie Sanders, a hematologist at the Hemophilia Center at Orthopaedic Hospital in Los Angeles. "Still, a few may have slipped through the cracks. We don't see patients with milder disorders as routinely, and now we're specifically looking for them to get them more information."

Women with a hemophiliac husband or boyfriend must clearly assume he is infected. The National Hemophilia Foundation, for example, advises that 5 percent of wives who sleep with their husbands without using condoms may become infected every year. Still, these women consistently have a lower rate of infection than the partners of men in other risk groups. As mentioned, some unknown aspect of hemophilia may inhibit or retard replication of the virus, making sexual transmission less likely.

Exceptional as hemophiliacs may be in some ways, they have provided us with a major lesson that we would do well to heed: the vast difference between diagnosed cases and levels of infection. Even though there are still only 267 hemophiliac diagnosed cases in the United States and even fewer cases diagnosed to date in European countries, hemophiliac men have the highest infection rate of any risk group. Without the research effort of testing, no one would have imagined that well over half of hemophiliacs in virtually the entire Western world are now HIV-infected. And we wouldn't have thought about preventing sexual transmission even in the one group that is easiest to reach and counsel.

The 404 male patients infected through blood transfusions are the next largest risk group, constituting another 1 percent of all diagnosed male Aids cases. Why twice as many men as women have transfusion-induced Aids is unknown. Since men and women receive almost the same number of units of blood annually, the risk should presumably be equal. "No one can explain the male predominance," says Dr. Julian B. Schorr, who analyzes Aids trends for the American Red Cross. "Maybe the men survive major surgery better to get Aids. Maybe more men were infected somehow. There's a continuing debate."

Compared to hemophiliacs, transfusion-infected men are an utterly undefined group. Almost all we know is that most of them are over age fifty and that heart surgery is the major procedure associated with male risk. But when the relevant studies are complete, it may well turn out that the greatest risk from blood transfusions was not for people who had surgery once but for those who required routine transfusion for various reasons. Results from testing at Columbia University, for example, suggest that a full 12 to 15 percent of chronically transfused sickle-cell anemia patients may have been infected. And, according to Dr. Charles H. Pegelow, Interim Director of the University of Miami Sickle Cell Center, early testing there also suggests that chronic transfusions increase the risk of HIV infection.

Not only don't we know *who* the transfusion-infected men are, no one knows how *many* there are. Various estimates have placed the total number of transfused men, women, and children who were infected with HIV but don't yet have Aids at 9,000 to 45,000. "I place it at about 25,000," says Dr. Tom Peterman, an epidemiologist at the CDC. "But, some 60 percent would have died already from their surgery or other natural causes. That leaves maybe 10,000 people still alive who were infected from transfusions."

The period of greatest risk for infection ended in the spring of 1983, when homosexuals and drug addicts were first warned not to donate blood. Given that about eighty million Americans had transfusions during the entire risk period from 1977 to 1985, when testing of donations almost fully eliminated infected blood from transfusions, if 25,000 people were infected, each transfusion patient ran a one in 3,200 risk of infection. This does not present a major prospect for sexual transmission; yet we do know that sexual transmissions have occurred. Women should be aware that the CDC has now recommended that all sexually active persons who had transfusions during the years of risk should be tested.

. . .

Men who inject drugs into their veins constitute 4,296 diagnosed Aids patients or 14 percent of the male total. Almost half are black, one-third are Hispanic, and 20 percent are white.

Of the estimated 500,000 drug addicts in the United States, three-quarters are men. Most live in New York, California, New Jersey, and Florida. But infection caused by drug abuse varies significantly by region, and it is directly connected to the practice of needle-sharing. In some communities, sharing needles is a general practice or custom; in others, it is not. In New York City, for example, where it is a crime to buy or even to carry a hypodermic needle without a doctor's prescription, many addicts shoot up in "galleries" in abandoned buildings where they can rent used needles. The result is that 65 percent or more of the city's drug addicts are infected, the highest rate in the nation. In New Jersey, infection seems to decrease directly with distance from New York City: 59 percent of the addicts in Newark are infected, but only 2 percent in southern New Jersey. In Washington, D.C., where just 5 percent of drug abusers say they share needles routinely, only 7 percent are infected. In New Orleans, where needle-sharing is uncommon, less than 1 percent of those tested in 1986 were infected.

Other reported American infection rates for addicts vary widely: 10 percent in San Francisco and 11 percent in Chicago, but 30 percent of those tested in Boston. As a rule, in most areas, including heavily infected New York, rates of infection for white addicts are about one-half to one-third of those for black and Hispanic addicts; the reason is simply that white addicts are the least likely to share needles. All told, these variations again show how essential it is for health authorities to publicize local Aids risks.

While, in the United States, local needle-sharing habits are good predictors of risk, the very different situation prevailing in Europe makes it clear that patterns of infection among drug addicts are still not fully understood. In most European countries addicts can easily buy sterile needles without a prescription—in some countries they can get them free—and shooting-galleries like those in New York are virtually unknown. Yet HIV infection, while evidently nonexistent among drug users in the major capitals before 1980, has now swept through European drug-injecting populations faster than in most areas of the United States. By 1986, 40 percent of intravenous drug users tested in Stockholm were infected, as were 41 percent in Edinburgh, 45 percent in Belgrade, 50 percent in West Berlin, 53 percent in Geneva, 64 percent in Paris, 64 percent in Madrid, and 71 percent in Barcelona.

Scientists still don't have a good explanation why drug-related infection occurred so quickly in Europe. As in the United States, heroin abuse is the main form of addiction among those infected; however, in other parts of the world that have yet to begin widespread testing of drug users, particularly in South America, we can probably expect to see large numbers of cocaine-injecting addicts join the ranks of the infected.

The risks of sexual transmission from intravenous-drug users are enormous. In the United States 80 percent of the nation's drug users have a wife or girlfriend who does not herself use drugs. And 67 percent of American women with sexually acquired Aids got it from a former or current addict. Although it is no secret that drug abusers are likely to be HIV-infected, many women seem to have major misunderstandings about who is and who isn't a drug addict. The common media image, of street junkies who shoot up heroin, does not address the fact that men can be "respectable" and still shoot drugs. At a program for heterosexual Aids patients and their families at the Montefiore Medical Center in the

Bronx, for example, almost half of the drug abusers are living in intact family households. "Many not only are married but also hold jobs and were shooting drugs recreationally only on weekends," emphasizes Monnie Callan, a social worker with the program. Nor do women seem to understand that needle-injected cocaine counts even if the user is an executive in a three-piece suit. " 'Recreational cocaine' is drug abuse also. It's sharing the needle with someone who's infected that matters," says Dr. Judith Cohen, co-director of AWARE in San Francisco, "not what's in the needle."

Then, too, women—and to some extent, drug addicts themselves—do not realize that the Aids-causing virus has been in the United States for at least a decade and that, consequently, even men who gave up drugs years ago can be infected. Indeed, in the first few years of the epidemic, HIV infection probably penetrated the drug-abusing population more rapidly than any other risk group except hemophiliacs. Retroactive analysis of preserved blood samples has shown that fully one-third of New York City addicts were already HIV carriers by 1979 and the Army has one well-documented case of a former New York City drug addict with Aids who had been infected in 1976. In New Haven, Connecticut, 10 percent of addicts tested between 1981 and 1983 had already been infected.

In sum, drug addicts may be the risk group that women think they can most easily identify—some disheveled guy nodding off in a doorway—but it's not that easy. Any man who has shot up drugs in the United States since 1976 (or, in Europe, since 1979) could be infected. Women cannot automatically tell who these men are.

Homosexual and bisexual men now constitute 71 percent of diagnosed male Aids cases in the United States, the largest group (21,279). This is an overwhelmingly white, middle-class population. Of these men, 20 percent have been married, and the average age at diagnosis is thirty-three, although, given the long incubation period for Aids, most of them certainly were much younger when they were infected.

Since most studies treat homosexual and bisexual men as a single group, it is hard to obtain separate information about bisexuals, the population that poses particular dangers to women. One of the few studies that does make the distinction reported that 31 percent of the black men and 20 percent of the Hispanic men officially assigned to the homosexual/bisexual group by the CDC say they are bisexual; but only 13 percent of the white patients say they are really bisexual. "We don't know why more blacks and Hispanics say they are bisexual," adds Dr. Roger Bakeman, professor of psychology at Georgia State University in Atlanta. "It could be a reporting bias or it could reflect behavior in the real world."

As with the drug-injecting population, infection varies greatly by place. In the United States, more than 75 percent of tested homosexuals and bisexuals in San Francisco are reported to be infected, as are at least 60 percent in New York City, 42 percent in Los Angeles, 30 percent in Boston, 15 percent in Minneapolis–St. Paul, and 8 percent in Ithaca, New York.

Reported infection rates from Europe include 32 percent in London, 31 percent in Amsterdam, 27 percent in Barcelona, 26 percent in Copenhagen, 13 percent in Rome, 13 percent in Madrid, 11 percent in Greece, 10 percent in Stockholm, and 6 percent in Hungary. In Vancouver, Canada, as many as 27 percent of tested homosexuals are positive; in Thailand, only 1 percent.

Since most testing is voluntary, however, it provides an infection rate only for men willing to identify themselves as homosexual or bisexual. By now, in the United States and increasingly in Europe, most such men are taking sexual precautions. Many probably do not sleep with either men or women without using a condom, if they still have direct intercourse at all. But nobody knows what percentage of homosexual and bisexual men do not identify themselves specifically by sexual orientation and, in particular, nobody has the least idea how many bisexual men there really are.

What Aids counselors already suspect, however, is that there are many more bisexuals than is generally acknowledged. While their actual rate of infection may well be lower than that of homosexual men, who sleep only with men, their internal denial may make them more dangerous, especially to women. Because of their double lives, they may be the most difficult group to reach and counsel. Aids counselors have noticed, for example, that with the proliferation of alternate test sites at which people can be tested with total anonymity, large numbers of bisexuals have finally been attracted to counseling. "I think we are just starting to understand the enormity of this problem," says Frank DeFrancesco, an Aids program counselor at the Connecticut State Department of Health Services. "In general, bisexual men have been able to lead two lives and keep them separate. Now, their coping mechanisms are no longer going to work. But how, for example, do they reveal their sexuality to a wife?"

Finally, it is important to understand that, by definition, this risk group includes *all* men with Aids who have had sex with another man even *once* since 1977, and therefore it clearly includes many men who are predominantly heterosexual. The experience of the Connecticut Regional Red Cross Blood Services, which collects blood for the entire state, addresses this point. In the fall of 1985, the Red Cross changed its guidelines to specify that no man who had sex—even once—with another man since 1977 should donate blood. The rate of infected donors, while not large, immediately plunged by 76 percent, from 34 to 8 per 100,000. "We know from comparing the infected groups before and after we changed our guidelines that the big group that was self-selecting out was men who'd had maybe one or two homosexual encounters in their entire lives, often five years or so ago, when they were adolescents," says Dr. Ritchard G. Cable, director of this blood program. "They hadn't paid attention to warnings that homosexuals shouldn't donate blood for the simple reason that they never thought of themselves as homosexual."

While the Connecticut figures suggest that the risk of infection from a few isolated adolescent experiments is low or, at least, was low five years ago, the extra risk to women is that these cases are so deceiving. When a man infected this way develops Aids, the Centers for Disease Control and local health departments alike classify him as homosexual/bisexual even though he has spent virtually his entire sexual life with women. To speak casually of the diagnosed cases as "71 percent homosexual," as so many health officials do, helps neither men nor women perceive the realities of risk.

The 613 men with Aids whom the Centers for Disease Control categorized as "purely" heterosexual constituted 2 percent of all American male cases by March 1987. These men were divided into two distinct groups. The first group comprised 500 immigrants from countries where Aids is now thought to be spread primarily by heterosexual intercourse and who told interviewers they had not used intravenous drugs or had a homosexual encounter since 1977. Most of these men are Haitian and African.

(In Europe, African immigrants also have a high rate of infection. But there is another distinct heterosexual group at risk for infection: European nationals who go to live or work in Africa for a few years, often to former colonies, and then return home. Of 81 heterosexual men who recently volunteered for testing when they returned to Denmark from Central Africa, seven [9 percent] were seropositive.)

For American-born men to be categorized as "heterosexual contact" cases, they must be non-drug-abusing, not have had homosexual intercourse since 1977, and know that they have slept with a woman at risk for Aids, such as a female drug user, a woman who has slept with a bisexual, or the former girlfriend of a hemophiliac. We can see how unrealistic—not to say silly—such criteria become. Considering how hard it is for a man to know these facts, especially about a woman he slept with five years ago, it is not surprising that only 113 men were categorized this way. To many critics, the figure indicated that a lot of heterosexual-contact Aids cases were just not being counted or were subsumed into other categories. Indeed, the only reason that as many as 113 were counted was that, in early 1986, the CDC reviewed several hundred "no known risk" cases reported during the first five years of the epidemic—the heterosexual category didn't exist at all then because heterosexuals weren't "supposed to get" Aids—and recategorized about one-third of them as heterosexual-contact Aids.

If the CDC figure was widely questioned, however, the claim of the New York City Department of Health that only *four* of the 9,000 Aids patients diagnosed in the city by spring 1987 were non–drug-using heterosexual males was so incredible that the Commissioner of Health finally had to say he would appoint a special panel to review the city's case-counting methods. One reason the city "found" so few heterosexual men was, almost certainly, a refusal to look for them. When a man who said he was heterosexual didn't know for sure whether any woman he had slept with was at risk for Aids, the Health Department made no attempt to test his present or past girlfriends for HIV infection. Instead, his case was simply assigned to the "no known risk" caseload.

This last official risk group of the Centers for Disease Control, "no known risk," in March 1987 contained 799 men, 3 percent of the diagnosed male cases. About half have not been interviewed yet. Others diagnosed in the early years of the epidemic will never be interviewed because they are no longer alive; some, although they deny it, no doubt have shot up drugs or had sex with a man. But a significant portion, who say they are heterosexual and haven't used intravenous drugs, are *not* classified as heterosexual-contact Aids cases only because they don't know "for sure" that they have ever slept with a woman at risk. "Virtually every man left in this group after investigation says he is heterosexual," adds Dr. Alan Lifson of the CDC. "Clearly, heterosexual transmission from an unrecognized source can be a reason for men to be in this group."

Looking at the diagnosed male cases, then, gives the impression that Aids is barely a heterosexual problem, much less an epidemic. But, once again, testing for HIV infection tells a far different story. The Armed Services' testing, still the only routine testing of younger Americans, gives some surprising indications about the spread of HIV. The most startling is the sex ratio of infection. As the male-female ratio of any venereal disease approaches one to one, the probability increases that it is being passed back and forth equally between men and women. Nationwide, among diagnosed Aids cases, there are 13 males for every female. Among infected Armed Services recruits, however, there are 2.5 men for every female; in New York City the ratio is now 1.3 to 1, or virtually equal. While we do not know that all the infected male recruits are heterosexual, we do know that this massive shift to women means that there is now an enormous group that can then transmit the virus heterosexually to men. There will be more and more infected men who, not having shot up drugs or had sex with another man, haven't the slightest idea that they have contracted HIV. Women should realize that, as this ratio equalizes, even the rather dim chance of protection offered by avoiding men in risk groups is fast disappearing.

The Armed Services results also show the geographical spread of Aids. There are already several areas of the country where the rate of infection is so high that *all* women have to consider Aids when starting a relationship. These include New York, northern New Jersey, Delaware, Maryland, and Washington, D.C.—what epidemiologists call the "I-95 corridor of infection," for the interstate highway that links the states. Other major HIV-infection centers include northern California, the Los Angeles area, the Las Vegas area, the Dallas-Houston area, Chicago, and southern Florida.

Moreover, the Armed Services screening shows that the epidemic is spreading to younger age groups. Half the diagnosed male patients with Aids (combining all "risk groups") are thirty-six or older; but the ages of highest infection for recruits are twenty-one to thirty-five. (About 85 percent of all venereal disease occurs in people under age thirty.) Has HIV reached college campuses or high schools? Leaving aside a few scattered case reports, nobody really knows. So far, few sixteen- to twenty-year-old men applying to the Armed Services have been infected, an encouraging circumstance that owes everything to luck and nothing to policy.

Finally, the Armed Services testing shows that, on average, 10 per 1,000 black male recruits and 3 per 1,000 white male recruits are infected. These figures are crucial to minority women, who must be aware of their extra risk. But it is also important to realize that as infection spreads, the rate starts to become equal by race. In New York City the figures already tell a different story: 12 per 1,000 black male recruits are HIV carriers, but so are 7 per 1,000 white male recruits. The figures strongly suggest that whites will soon constitute an increasing portion of the diagnosed heterosexual-contact cases.

What does all this mean for women? First of all, they must gauge their risks by looking at local statistics of infection. No matter how many health officials point to risk groups, and diagnosed cases, what counts most is the much larger, much broader, spreading infection. As the sex ratio of infection equalizes, the epidemic is rapidly becoming heterosexual, and all comfortable reliance on risk groups for self-protection is invalidated.

On the whole, infection is greatest in urban areas, although some small towns—Belle Glade, Florida, is the best known—also have high levels of heterosexual infection. At present, black and Hispanic women, including those in the vastly different Hispanic communities of New York, California, and Florida, face a much greater risk than white women; but the Armed Services testing, particularly in large cities, shows that white women are starting to become equally infected. At present, half of women diagnosed are thirty-five or older, but the greatest risk of infection is rapidly shifting to women under thirty-five.

To women throughout the United States, the most salient aspect of "Aids counting" is the way the established risk groups have deceived them about the real dangers. These groupings serve only to perpetuate the myth that most men with Aids spent their entire lives hermetically isolated from any sexual contact with women; and the categories strain in every way against counting a man as heterosexual. They have provided a psychological and often publicly stated excuse for officials not to bother with the prevention efforts and measures that are routine for other epidemics, and, unfortunately, "risk groups" are becoming the standard way of categorizing and thinking about Aids in other countries as well.

For women the result can be, quite simply, lethal. Certainly, any woman who looked at the four lone heterosexual males listed in the New York City caseload, for example, and concluded that only four men in the city could have given her Aids, would be taking her life in her hands—as so many New York women have done.

Chapter Three

Personal Prevention

"You know that old saying, 'Love is blind.' If I had one thing to say to women, I would say that, today, love should be alert."—Mary, a woman with Aids

Clearly, we must do everything possible to protect everyone from getting Aids. At present, however, women will find that they have to depend largely on measures they can take for themselves. The dilemma is only too obvious: making love is a mutual act, but Aids has not yet been understood as a mutual disease of heterosexuals—"a regular, old-fashioned venereal disease," to use Dr. Redfield's term. Most heterosexual men probably don't dream they could be at risk; and public education has been so meager that even some men who are technically in a risk group for infection—those who gave up intravenous drugs years ago, for example, or had a few homosexual encounters—still don't realize that they should take precautions against spreading Aids to women.

Given these circumstances, every woman should be

aware of two immediate means of personal protection. The first is physical protection: using condoms and "safer sex" techniques that prevent semen from getting into her body, whether her vagina, rectum, or mouth. The second is emotional protection: knowing a man well and trusting him before sleeping with him. These approaches are not mutually exclusive. Discussing the reasons for safer sex will involve couples in serious conversations that may not otherwise occur when people are first dating, and the very act of using condoms may introduce a shared sense of responsibility that is often missing with other methods of birth control.

With risks as well as fears varying so much throughout the United States, each woman will come to her own conclusions about measures for protection. But as Dr. Judith Cohen, co-director of AWARE, urges, "all women today, in their sexual behavior, have to start considering their responsibilities to themselves and their partners."

The exhortation "just use condoms" has been a major slogan of Aids prevention for women. But, as always, there's a big difference between slogans and education. Women need to understand not only how to use condoms but also how to talk about using them. Not surprisingly, the biggest obstacle is that many men still don't realize the need for Aids prevention or, even if they do, have never learned how to put condoms on correctly. This is essential: the safety of condoms depends on using and handling them correctly.

By now, all types of condoms, including latex, lambskin, and "synthetic skin" brands, have been rigorously tested in laboratories. None of them permits the virus to seep through, even when a heavy concentration is left in the condom for hours. A few medical authorities have been reluctant to recommend lambskin condoms, which many men prefer as "more natural," because hepatitis B virus can seep through them. However, there is currently no evidence that they permit HIV seepage. "Hepatitis B," Dr. Cohen points out, "is a much more infectious virus."

Nonetheless, given rips, spills, and human error, we cannot expect this perfect record in the laboratory to be matched in bed, although how unmatched it will be is hard to say. The Miami Clinical Research Unit has published the only information available to date on the use of condoms in real life. Among the first sixteen couples in which infected husbands routinely used condoms to have intercourse with previously uninfected wives, two women became infected within a year. What makes these results hard to interpret is that both men had already been diagnosed with Aids, and one couple had continued to have unprotected oral sex, and the wife had swallowed semen.

In looking at the 12 percent rate of transmission for these couples, it is important to remember that, by comparison, 86 percent of women in the Miami study who were sexually exposed to the virus during this period contracted HIV when their husbands did not use condoms—a very significant increase. What is especially significant is that the 12 percent rate of transmission in the Miami study fits exactly with the "typical" 10 to 15 percent failure rate of condoms in preventing pregnancy. We know from long experience that this typical rate can be slashed to 1 percent when couples really understand how to use condoms, avoiding the simple but common errors that permit leakage and spills, and use spermicidal contraceptives such as foams, jellies, and creams in combination with condoms. There is every reason to think that HIV transmission, even within the steady exposure of marriage or long-term relationships, can be reduced in the same way.

Sunny Rumsey, an educator for the New York City Department of Health, is well qualified by good humor and clear language to teach people how condoms are put on. Her first point is that women, too, have to start thinking about condoms long before the lights go out. If they're not familiar with them, they should read the instructions before stepping out the door for a date, and they should carry condoms with them. "If you leave them back in your bedroom," she emphasizes, "you may not have them when you want them. Next comes opening the package. Open it carefully. You'd be surprised how many people tear the condom, either with their fingernails or teeth, when they're opening the package.

"When the condom goes on, the penis has to be partly or fully erect. If your partner hasn't started to get an erection, the condom won't stay, and that's why the condom ends up on the floor so often. It should absolutely go on before he puts his penis inside you. Don't 'have a little sex' first and then put on the condom.

"If a woman puts the condom on a man, this, of course, makes it more erotic and he's more willing to use it. Some condoms have an extra reservoir tip at the end to hold the semen. If you're using a brand that doesn't, leave about a half-inch empty at the end when you put the condom on the penis. Then press out the air in the built-in tip—or the extra half-inch that you leave—by pressing it flat with your fingers. The reason you don't want this tip filled with air is to leave enough room for the semen to collect. You then roll the condom all the way down so it covers the penis. It unrolls from the outside, so if you're having trouble getting it to unroll, you've got it inside out.

"Now, after you make love and he ejaculates, a lot of people like to stay right there, close to each other. But you can't just do that. As the penis starts to soften, the condom can drop off. He should pull out right afterward, holding the rim of the condom to make sure it doesn't come off or spill. After you've used a condom once, throw it out! It's not a wash-and-wear product or a family heirloom."

Women often find that the chief obstacle to using condoms is getting men to agree. Contraceptive pills and IUDs have shifted the responsibility for birth control almost entirely to women for twenty years, and antibiotics have made venereal disease far less frightening to men. It is not always easy for men to realize that the need for condoms is as great in 1987 as it was when syphilis was a potentially fatal disease. Some men may react indignantly, or even angrily, to the suggestion of condoms. (Two favorite excuses, says Ms. Rumsey, are "I'd like to, but none of them fit me," and "Weren't you just talking about trust? Don't you trust me?") A calm, affectionate approach that does not imply that the man is a skulking disease carrier will help. The simple statement, "I like you, but I would enjoy it so much more with this protection," makes the point. The reply to the claim that condoms diminish sex is that worrying diminishes sex.

Ms. Rumsey urges women not to leave their first "condom conversation" with a man to the last minute. "You want to bring this up well before the clothes are flying into the air or even before you get into each other's arms," she says. "It's very, very hard to have a discussion then. What are you going to do if he says, 'Come on. Let's just do it this once and we'll talk about condoms next time'?" Making condoms sensual also helps to make them attractive. If a woman buys four or five brands of condoms and says, "Let's try them all and see which one we like best," that would be almost irresistible. On the other hand, the point at which she feels she is becoming single-handedly responsible for two people's health, and the man is not being gracious or cooperative at all, may be the point at which she decides not to proceed with the relationship. After all, millions of men throughout the world use condoms routinely. It really shouldn't be such a big deal. And it is for the man's protection, too.

There are a few other things to know about condoms:

they should fit snugly (brands vary somewhat in shape and size), they come in black and white skin shades, and they can be either lubricated or unlubricated. Very occasionally, a man or woman may have slight itchy reactions to lubricated condoms that also contain spermicides. In that case, even though the extra spermicide makes the condom safer, try another brand. If you want to add your own lubricant (it goes on the outside of the condom and eases entry of the penis into the vagina), don't use an oil-based one like baby oil or Vaseline with a latex condom; these lubricants cause latex to disintegrate. Instead, use K-Y jelly.

Beyond the small amount of spermicide contained in some lubricated condoms, however, there is the real safety to be gained by also using female "barrier" contraceptives—foams, jellies, and creams—that contain HIV-killing spermicides. In laboratory experiments in the United States, the spermicide nonoxynol-9 has been shown to rapidly kill HIV and most other organisms that cause sexually transmitted disease. This spermicide, which sometimes appears on product labels in the guise of its totally unpronounceable chemical name—p-Diisobutylphenoxypolyethoxyethanol—is contained in most spermicidal products sold in the United States. Some common products are: Intercept, Encare Inserts, Delfin Foam, Koromex Cream or Gel, Conceptrol Gel, Ramses Gel, and VCF Contraceptive Film. In France, tests with a widely used European spermicide, benzalkonium chloride, have shown that it, too, kills HIV.

While condoms alone have a 10 to 15 percent failure rate in preventing pregnancy, the addition of a spermicidal contraceptive reduces the rate to 5 percent. But this still includes failures resulting from mistakes, like putting on the condom incorrectly or "having just a little sex" before bothering with the condom or spermicide. Used absolutely correctly, the combination of condom and spermicide is 99 percent effective against pregnancy.

Whether it is that effective against HIV, we do not know, having no research; but we have reason to think so. In studies, women who use spermicides sustain low rates of other venereal infections; certainly, it has turned out for gonorrhea and syphilis and a number of other diseases that the ability of spermicides to kill organisms has helped provide protection in real life. Indeed, condoms used with spermicides will have gigantic health benefits for women aside from Aids prevention; almost overnight, this combination could terminate the chlamydia and gonorrhea epidemics that have caused massive outbreaks of pelvic inflammatory disease (PID) and left many American women, particularly younger ones, infertile. "In the women's health movement, we have strongly recommended the condom and spermicide combination for years, both because it is so protective and because it involves men and women equally in contraception," comments Andrea Eagan, a women's health writer and organizer.

Between foams, jellies, and creams, foam may be best. In *Women's Health Care,* birth-control expert Barbara Seaman reports that "foams such as Emko and the newer foaming suppositories such as Encare and Semicid . . . disperse better." Whether a diaphragm with jelly or a vaginal sponge helps protect against HIV infection, effective as they are in preventing pregnancy, is unknown. Let's remember, there's a big difference. The diaphragm and jelly block sperm from leaving the vagina to reach the Fallopian tubes and fertilize an egg. But HIV in semen is infectious while still in the vagina. Logically, then, because foams coat the vaginal lining with spermicide, they protect better against HIV. Both foam and the newer foaming suppositories are quite easy to use; a woman just pushes the suppository into her vagina with her finger. Nonetheless, until the effectiveness of foam as an HIV block is understood, women should not depend on it as their only protection against Aids.

Given the distinct value of such measures, many educators now recommend that all women starting a relationship insist at least on condoms. In areas where Aids is spreading rapidly this is unquestionably excellent advice; elsewhere it may not be quite as urgent. In other words, a woman being courted by a widower in Iowa might think about Aids and then dismiss the need for a condom, while a woman in Miami starting her fifth fling of the year would be foolish to do the same.

Just as the choices about using condoms, and the supplement of foam, will vary according to the Aids risks of where and how women live, so their choices may change when they know for certain that a man is infected. Some women may still decide that they want to continue a sexual relationship, relying on the protection of a condom and foam. For other women, particularly those who have young children, even a 1 percent risk will be too great, and they may decide to follow safer sex practices.

"Safer sex" is rather loosely defined as sensual pleasure without direct intercourse. (Because the various Aids definitions are still evolving, using condoms is sometimes referred to as safer sex. In this discussion, however, the term excludes intercourse with condoms.) Couples are advised to kiss, hug, be cozy, and use their hands; among the many such couples studied at the Miami Clinical Research Unit, no wife of an infected husband has yet become infected from kissing, hugging, masturbating him, or being masturbated by him.

This still leaves out the question of oral sex, which some educators include as a safer sex practice (others do not). There are no studies at all of oral sex as a means of viral transmission between heterosexuals (the safer-sex couples studied in Miami did not engage in oral sex). As mentioned, however, a number of studies now suggest that homosexuals who have confined their sexual activity to oral sex have not become infected with HIV. Still, because there is not enough evidence to make total guarantees, and because of the high concentration of HIV in semen, some Aids educators advise women against performing oral sex on an infected man, unless condoms are used. There are also no guarantees about cunnilingus, but, again, it seems extremely unlikely that an infected man could transmit HIV to a woman by performing oral sex on her; since the amount of HIV in saliva is so small, mouth-to-vagina contact, on the evidence so far, appears to be safe.

Safer-sex guidelines should also be considered when a woman is the infected partner. In that case, not having vaginal intercourse would preclude one form of infection by eliminating contact with vaginal secretions. A man performing oral sex on an infected woman would come in contact with vaginal secretions, but this, too, seems a very unlikely mode of transmission. Vagina-to-mouth transmission of other venereal disease is rare. Dr. Barbara Herbert, of the Women and Aids Project in Washington, D.C., points out that there are only two recorded cases in the entire medical literature of a man contracting gonorrhea from oral sex with a woman, and gonorrhea is much easier to get than Aids. Nonetheless, the "extra" concentration of HIV in menstrual blood may make oral sex more dangerous when a woman has her period. Similarly, if an infected woman's partner has bleeding gums or sores in his mouth, that could also increase his chances of contracting HIV from oral sex, although this, too, is an unknown. To a large degree, then, until there is conclusive research, people will have to make up their own minds about the safety of oral sex.

The rare cases of lesbian transmission have highlighted safer-sex concerns about oral sex and blood. While lesbians have gotten Aids from infected transfusions and drug abuse, it seemed at first that the female sex partners of these women might be entirely protected from sexual transmission: kissing and mouth-to-vagina contact, which are major aspects of les-

bian sexuality, appeared to be quite unlikely means of transmission. However, at least two cases of viral transmission
between female sex partners have now been reported. In the
best-studied case, the women had oral contact during menstruation, passed sex toys (dildos) back and forth, and caused
vaginal bleeding—separate from menstruation—by their sexual activities. It appears quite possible that blood, whether
exchanged orally or by an infected dildo pressed against tears
in the vagina, may have been the source of transmission. This,
of course, is important not only for lesbians but for everyone.
Sex toys—whether dildos, vibrators, or anything else—
should never be passed from an infected person to someone
else. And again, infected people should remember that blood
is potentially dangerous, especially during sex.

Some lesbian health centers have issued extensive safer
sex guidelines that emphasize avoiding vagina-vulva rubbing,
being careful with sex toys, and taking other precautions if
one partner is at risk for infection. The real argument has
arisen over dental dams. Dental dams are the rectangular
strips of latex used by dentists to cover the inside of the
mouth and isolate a particular tooth. They can be bought at
medical-supply stores and some drugstores. Lightly inserted
as a lining for the opening of the vagina, they function as the
woman's equivalent of a condom for oral sex, blocking the
passage of both saliva and vaginal secretions.

Some safer-sex pamphlets, whether for lesbians or for
other women, now recommend that dental dams be used routinely—just like condoms. Since there is no conclusive evidence that HIV is spread by oral sex—as long as blood isn't
involved—there is no indication that dental dams are generally needed. Such recommendations raise important issues in
the psychology of Aids prevention. Obviously, all women,
lesbian or not, should do what makes them feel comfortable:
if they have an infected partner, they may simply *feel* safer

with a dental dam, and that in itself can be important. But other women find dental dams very intimidating. And any interruption of ongoing education about real Aids risks for still hypothetical ones can be counterproductive. One Aids educator, for example, tried to introduce dental dams to a group of women in drug treatment—women with enough problems just trying to talk to men about condoms. They found the whole idea so annoying and outlandish that they lost interest in the prevention lecture altogether. In other words, we can have too much Aids education as well as too little.

Despite the apparent novelty of the term, many safer sex practices are just what used to be done on old-fashioned dating. Kissing, hugging, and coziness are simply what people used to do for weeks, months, or years before intercourse. As the available answer when a husband or wife is known to be infected, safer sex is a specific response to a threatening situation. Safer sex is also part of the caring approach to Aids prevention, which involves building an enduring and close relationship before and apart from intercourse. Despite an antiseptic new name, safer sex practices are nothing new. They are a way of being physically close while endowing sex with a certain sense of grace and wonder that many people may rejoice in rediscovering.

All told, the first immediate step in personal protection for women, the use of condoms and foam, provides a significant defense against Aids. But personal protection must include more than a few questions and a request to get out a condom. Relations between men and women are not that simple, and it is hard to care about strangers. Indeed, the process of getting to know each other that Aids will necessarily impose on men and women may well lead to greater care and responsibility between the sexes. Twenty years of birth-control pills and sexual revolution have combined to cast women in a role of sexual availability that can be bitterly unpleasant. The question of how women can have sexual equality without being sexually exploited has troubled us for two decades.

The optimistic view of Aids prevention is that we will now have to answer this question—and answer it by accenting the values of truth and trust in relationships. "Aids will mean that women can expect to really know men before they make love," states Dr. Joyce Wallace, a Manhattan researcher who also treats many Aids patients. "It will also mean that they can expect much more loyalty."

Yet, hopeful views are not immediate solutions. Aids prevention will require serious, careful, and sustained thought about approaches that bring the sexes closer together. Aids cannot become a substitute for dealing with men. Any woman, for instance, who used the pre-pill excuse of fear of pregnancy for not sleeping with a man—sometimes mumbled as "But I don't wanna get pregnant"—knows what a lame way this is to talk about human relations. An excuse of this kind in no way addresses the questions that come up at the beginning of any relationship. Does the woman feel comfortable about having a sexual relationship? Does she want to date or be married? Does she feel pushed by the man? Does she simply not know if she wants to go out with him at all? In the same way, a mumbled "But I don't wanna get Aids" will not help women build a relationship to which they can entrust not just their physical health but also their emotions.

Women need not use their concern about Aids as an excuse to turn down sex at the beginning of a relationship. "I'd like to get to know you" not only has the sufficiency of truth but, most important, it speaks to a man as a person and not just as a medical history. After she knows him well enough to talk comfortably, and if she wishes to continue dating him, a woman can bring up the subject of Aids. The question, of course, is how. Some health educators recommend the direct approach: be as pleasant, simple, and non-threatening as possible—but also be straightforward. "There's just no way to bring up a subject like this and pretend that you're not," says Judy Norsigian, a co-author of *Our Bodies, Ourselves.* By now, any man who is even slightly aware of the disease should expect to discuss the subject, but many don't. Aids counselors remark again and again that heterosexual men seem to have the greatest trouble of all in talking about Aids.

Perhaps the most nonthreatening way is for a woman simply to state, "I'm sure you know that people are worried about Aids. I think we should talk about it. I know it's not easy, but from what I've learned, most people don't fully understand the risks. They think you just have to be gay or an addict. But even a guy who shot up drugs a few times or got seduced by some guy when he was a teenager might have a small risk."

Many conversations will stop here. Either the man will say that he knows these risks don't exist for him, or some hesitation in his manner will suggest that perhaps they do. "Use your instincts," advises Susan Rosenthal, Director of the New York City Aids Hotline, "If something doesn't seem quite right, is it worth it to worry?" Many conversations will also stop right there because men can get angry, and this is obviously a good moment for reassurance and for acknowledging that you, too, as a woman, have Aids responsibilities: "Look, I like you. And I've had to think about whether I've had any risks in my own life. I don't think I have, but instead of taking any chances, *I'm* willing to use condoms and foam. I couldn't live with myself knowing I wasn't careful about *you.* There. My cards are on the table."

No matter how caring and tactful a woman is, however, some men will put an abrupt end to the conversation. Either

they will have realized they have a risk and refuse to talk
about it, or they will refuse to talk—period. While this may
be hard to accept if you like someone, it is bound to happen
sometimes. If, in addition to walking out, a man tries to make
you feel guilty or acts nasty, remember that he is not reacting
to you but to the idea of discussing Aids. The topic makes
some people, men and women alike, feel very threatened and
act irrationally the first time someone insists it must be discussed. So don't be upset yourself. Call up a girlfriend, have
a cup of coffee, go to a movie, and forget the whole incident.

A man who admits to having a risk, or realizes that he
might have a risk, is telling you something very difficult,
totally confidential, and obviously requiring the greatest compassion, affection, and reassurance. One possible solution in
this situation is to suggest he take a test for infection; at this
stage in the epidemic the chances of infection for most people
are still small enough that the worry about Aids far exceeds
the bother and anxiety of taking the test. Unfortunately, some
risks, including promiscuity and having slept with prostitutes,
are so undefined that it is hard to advise people with anything
near the clarity and information they want. The bottom line,
again, is that testing will relieve most people of a brutal worry,
while giving them a good opportunity to be counseled about
avoiding Aids risks in the future. Why not go with him and
get an HIV test yourself? This recommendation may seem
farfetched now, but it is not. Although testing is still not
common outside of major risk groups, there are already
signs—legislative proposals for widespread testing and increased demand at test sites—that more and more people consider testing a personal responsibility.

The direct approach has much to recommend it, not the
least being that it undoubtedly establishes communication in
the relationship, for better or worse. Yet there are other ways
to get an idea of a man's background. "The best way to get

information is to talk about yourself first," Emily Prager recently advised in a "Post-Aids Dating Guide." In other words, the story about the first time you smoked marijuana could encourage your date to tell you about his own drug use, including the important point of whether he has ever injected drugs. Or, simply saying that you have changed your dating habits in reaction to Aids may lead him to talk about his own.

Another way of getting to know men is to be selective. A bachelor and financier in New York City observes that women now not only often refuse to make love until they know someone well—"It used to be on two dates and now it's fifteen"—but also that both men and women are confining their love life to a smaller circle of people. "A lot of people just won't ask direct questions," he says. "In particular, women are very reluctant to imply that a man is gay. So they get around it by going out with people they already know or whose past they can ask their own friends about."

Of course, women will wonder how honest men are being even when they are having an apparently open and frank discussion. To some extent, honesty depends on awareness. Hemophiliacs are the male risk group that is most educated about Aids. Considerable evidence also suggests that drug addicts—or, at least, drug addicts in treatment—are unexpectedly honest and careful about Aids. Many drug users in treatment, and even some not in treatment, have been counseled about Aids risks and safer sex practices; they have also had the chilling experience of watching friends and acquaintances die a terrible death. Most who have been tested and know they are infected appear to routinely use condoms. "Certainly we can say that a lot of male drug addicts understand this disease better than most middle-class men," states Sam Friedman, of Narcotic and Drug Research, Inc., a New York State–affiliated research group.

By contrast, Aids counselors do not expect a high level

of honesty from bisexual men—at least, not yet. This group can range from men who are essentially married homosexuals—they may have a wife and family but lead their own sexual life primarily with other men—to bisexuals who are equally interested in both sexes. A major problem is that so many bisexual men remain in hiding that they simply haven't talked about Aids to anyone, a process that enormously inhibits prevention. "It's so devastating to these men to acknowledge this part of themselves," says Jill Strawn, R.N., an Aids risk-reduction counselor in the New Haven, Connecticut, Department of Health, "that women have to be aware that they may not get a true answer." Ms. Strawn points out that if these men engaged only in oral sex with other men, their Aids risk would be very low; but many don't know that because they are too petrified and conflicted to simply get some facts. "It's too bad," she adds, "that more of them don't come in for counseling to find out what their true risks are."

And honesty is not the only problem. Most men's understanding of their own risks still remains so cloudy that women cannot always be sure they have learned the truth even when the conversation is candid. Heterosexual men, in particular, many have no idea that they could have contracted HIV, and men who will be honest about what they have done recently will dismiss from their minds what they did in the past. It is not surprising that 11 percent of women with diagnosed Aids simply do not know how they contracted the disease. These women probably did sleep with an infected man who may not have realized his risk at the time.

Even with all the male misunderstanding at present, women should not conclude that men don't want to be responsible about Aids. The results from intensely educating hemophiliacs and drug addicts show just the opposite, and most men in both groups are heterosexual. Clearly, awareness and knowledge are the keys to responsibility.

The situation of married women who think their husbands may be at risk for infection requires special attention: these women find themselves in a wilderness of emotions that single women do not have to confront. A wife who suspects her husband has a risk he hasn't told her about may be facing a distraught man eager to be responsible but frightened that it is too late. He may be so afraid of having already hurt his wife that he sees no choice but to go on lying to himself and to her. Yet he may still be sending a strong signal that he wants to talk. One social worker describes the case of a former drug user who had simply refused to make love with his wife for six months; in marriage counseling the real issue, his fear of transmitting Aids to her, finally surfaced. Affection and patience, particularly the reassurance that "I'm not going to leave you," may almost immediately give men who want to talk the courage to start.

The emotional stress of dealing with HIV infection in a marriage is usually quieted over time, and in fact, very few wives do leave an infected or sick husband. At first, however, this stress can be so intense that a woman may fear that forcing her husband to look at his denial may end the marriage. Some women have even reported violence.

Before beginning the conversation, a wife may wish to call her local Aids hotline for advice (see Appendix). If violence seems possible, she may be wise to try to bring her husband for counseling rather than talk to him by herself first. (If he won't go, she should go herself.) In any of these situations, counseling is invaluable because it provides a much clearer idea of the real risks. In the end, only a wife can judge how she might best talk to her husband; yet, even people who do not generally believe in counseling should realize that Aids is profoundly different from other problems. A woman in this situation will probably not want to talk to the friends or relatives she usually looks to for solace or advice. Yet she needs comfort, and she needs facts.

. . .

Personal protection against Aids—the correct use of condoms and foam, and relationships built on honesty and awareness —is just common sense. Its advantages in physical and emotional well-being make it the obvious thing to do. Yet incredibly enough, for all the talk about Aids, personal protection is still not widely practiced. To the considerable shock of health officials, neither gonorrhea nor syphilis, the two most immediately measurable venereal infections, decreased in the United States in 1986. (The 850,000 reported cases of gonorrhea, in fact, are estimated to represent only half of the actual cases.) Since separate studies of homosexuals, who as a group are highly aware of safer sex practices, show that their gonorrhea rate has plummeted, the overall figures mean that gonorrhea among heterosexuals has almost certainly increased, indicating no major effort by sexually active heterosexuals to protect themselves from anything.

"Wherever other VD goes, Aids is bound to follow," says Dr. Keith Henry, Medical Director of the St. Paul Department of Health Aids Unit. "The heterosexual population is right in line. It's like knowing the storm in the mountains is going to come your way."

How is it possible, in a country inundated with almost daily reports about a fatal disease, that so little appears to have changed? There are several reasons. The experience with male risk groups shows that *direct* education of men can work very well, yet the scanty education so far directed at heterosexuals has presented Aids prevention as something for which women are solely responsible: women are supposed to get men to use condoms and to figure out which men are bisexual or drug abusers. As long as health officials fail to discuss Aids as a heterosexual issue, leaving women in the absurd position of getting condoms on men, we can hardly expect general progress.

Then, too, fear and death are still the focus of most public discussions about Aids. This theme is epitomized in recent condom advertisements that feature a distressed woman under the headline message, "I like sex, but not enough to die for it." Considering that the combination of sex and death is precisely what leads people to deny their own risk of Aids in the first place, it is not surprising that this morbid approach seems to have largely backfired.

We are still fumbling for ways to talk about Aids, but dwelling on the negative does not inspire millions of people to action. Advice that leaves people alone with condoms in their hands and terror in their hearts is not enough to combat this epidemic. As we fight Aids, we should take for our example the spiritual and moral energy of the great social movements of the past thirty years—civil rights, environmentalism, feminism. To inspire the massive social change that Aids prevention requires, we must look for goals that are both spiritually and literally life-affirming. But mass movements don't occur spontaneously, and this brings up public education.

Chapter Four

Public Imperatives:
Education and Testing

"Education about Aids should not be thought of in terms of a single packet of information to be delivered to the appropriate recipients, but in terms of maintaining behavior change over an indefinite time period."—S. R. Friedman, D. C. Des Jarlais, J. L. Sotheran, Health Education Quarterly

The most successful Aids-education program for women in the United States is AWARE, based in San Francisco, and the principles it has evolved for reaching and counseling women are worth looking at closely. "Before we started, we asked a lot of women's groups and community groups to give us their advice," says Dr. Cohen, the co-director. "The main thing we learned was that women were very opposed to any program that was linked to existing Aids clinics. Women perceived them as being for gays and drug abusers and, if they were municipal Aids clinics, not places they could necessarily trust. So, we put four of our testing sites in public or community-run clinics that had women's programs but not other Aids programs. The fifth site is a hotel frequented by prostitutes.

Prostitutes really did not want to go to any city clinic. Most important, since we did listen, we got a reputation from the beginning as being people you could talk to."

The main mission of AWARE is to counsel about sexual transmission; as a priority, it offers direct testing and advice to women in two categories: those who have slept with a man they know is at risk for Aids, and women who had slept with five or more men in the San Francisco area in the previous three years. "I don't know that I'd be that worried about women in Kansas City who had five or more partners," Dr. Cohen adds. AWARE assures these women absolute confidentiality; when they first come for testing, they are assigned a number and not asked their names. And by offering preventive counseling, and the promise of continued medical and psychological support if they test positive, AWARE attracted more than 400 women for testing by mid-1986 (4 percent were HIV-infected, a figure that increased to 5.5 percent in early 1987).

Equally important, AWARE became a catalyst for women's education in San Francisco, helping a full range of women's groups form educational programs and seminars of their own. Together with Coyote, the prostitutes' rights organization, AWARE is working closely to help the sex industry become a source of Aids prevention in San Francisco. Yet, until AWARE made Aids a specifically female concern, none of this could have happened. Even in San Francisco, where epidemiologists estimate that three thousand women may have contracted HIV from bisexual men alone, women who were eager for help and counseling still would not go to a general Aids clinic.

The combination of education and testing offered by AWARE is ideal: it provides a setting to ask personal questions, an information resource for local education campaigns, and the immediate and confidential testing that is essential for controlling the epidemic. The services it provides are necessary throughout the country to help women understand and deal with Aids.

Outside the major Aids areas, the need for education is obvious. In Minnesota, for example, Dr. Keith Henry, medical director of the Aids Unit for the St. Paul Department of Health, was startled to find that even women who were members of local sex, or "swingers', " clubs did not worry about Aids despite routinely having intercourse with twenty-five or more men every few months. He began to test St. Paul and Minneapolis swingers after nurses at the local venereal disease clinic pointed out that members of two local clubs had been steady clients for other infections for years. Fifty-nine women agreed to testing; two were seropositive. (They had probably been infected by two bisexual members who had moved and could not be tested.) None of the heterosexual men in the club, including the husband of one infected woman, was yet infected. "What was really shocking and disappointing was that the vast majority of these sexually sophisticated people did not see themselves at risk for Aids," says Dr. Henry. "The women knew there were bisexual men in the club, but they hadn't really thought about it. It was 'their' club, and they knew the men. Aids was something that happened to gays or to bisexuals they didn't know. Nobody used condoms."

But even in the suburbs of New York, women at risk—not to mention women in general—are still blind to the realities of Aids. "The lack of knowledge in our female population is astounding and appalling," comments Leslie Stein, Director of Education for the Mid-Hudson Valley Aids Task Force, which serves seven counties north of New York City. "So many people in our area moved here to get away from urban problems that they don't want to think about Aids at all. They don't know or 'forget' their husband might have abused drugs. When you tell one of these women she's infected, she may refuse to believe you." All told, Boston, San Francisco, and Los Angeles are the only American cities with major Aids-education programs directed at women—in all cases, programs started by community groups, not by the health department. In New York City, which has the greatest number of female cases, the Department of Health still had not created a special educational pamphlet for women by the end of 1986.

Yet for all the failure to educate women about Aids, a disturbing new trend has started to emerge. As the situation gets more serious, some health officials—and a growing number of "instant experts"—expect that somehow the solution will come by making women responsible for stopping heterosexual Aids all by themselves. Both the best and the worst educational materials now echo this theme. The film *Sex, Drugs, and Aids,* originally made for the New York City Board of Education, is being shown to high-school students throughout the country. As generally effective and forceful as this film may be, the "condom section," amazingly, shows three girls chatting about where to buy them and why they should be used. Never are teenaged boys shown talking about condoms, nor does any boy ever make the simple statement that boys have some responsibility toward girls. Also, for some reason, in a film made for a school system that is 80 percent black, Hispanic, and Asian, all three girls are white.

For adults, there is the television version of the "I don't want to die" campaign. Conceived by New York advertising personality Jerry Della Femina this commercial, too, features a woman, again white, discussing the virtues of condoms but never the importance of mutual responsibility. Della Femina has promoted himself as "performing a public service" for having created an ad that thoroughly relieves men of any role in Aids prevention. Most major network stations still refuse to broadcast condom ads or public service announcements. But eventually they will have to give in. Will the way to make Aids prevention "permissible" be to make it cute, blue-eyed, and female? "About the worst block we're having with Aids prevention in the United States is the television and advertising image of women as 'cleaners,' " says Dr. Henry. "They can be shown waxing floors, cleaning furniture, or talking about tampons and vaginal douches because the role of women in TV ads is to keep things clean. Yet condom ads directed at men can't be shown."

Let's get serious. If the public expression of Aids prevention becomes a group of women sitting around and talking about condoms, we are headed toward failure. Condom campaigns resoundingly directed at women not only ignore the biological fact that it is men who wear condoms, but they also dismiss the emotional truth of Aids prevention: it must be a mutual undertaking. As the remarkable health organizations built by gay men have thoroughly learned, condoms are merely a physical means of Aids prevention, not a motivating spirit or force. Aids prevention, as we have seen, also entails communication, honesty, responsibility—and love. And these are "products" that can certainly be advertised on television with condom talk.

Indeed, condom ads and effective Aids education will have to confront the whole way that Americans deal—or fail to deal—with sex. It is a curious fact that we probably have more "public sex" than any nation in the world. Sex sells products, stares from billboards, pours from magazine racks, and, in the quiet of Sunday evenings, crackles from advice shows on the radio. Yet compared to this public noise, our private communication about sex is singularly limited. We have no real sex education and, even under the threat of Aids, we have yet to find ways of talking about sex as a real experience and now a real concern. Our efforts at discourse are "usually inarticulate and remote from individual experience," comments Cindy Patton in *Sex and Germs: The Politics of Aids.* "The most intelligent statements are couched in terms so far removed from how real people think about sex that they become meaningless."

The reasons for this mumbling in such a publicly sexualized atmosphere are complex. Some trace it to a lingering Puritan heritage; others consider the media noise itself to be the problem. Perhaps it is precisely because we are so inundated with commercialized sex that it has become virtually impossible to talk about sex as a genuinely human experience.

In any case, our failure to do so has seriously compromised possibilities for Aids education at every level. The many public figures who are never at a loss for words in a crisis are now strangely tongue-tied. Indeed, for any public figure in America to discuss sex as something that affects you and me and them—as distinct from talk-show recitals of affairs and adventures and techniques—is almost unimaginable. In England, Prime Minister Margaret Thatcher, the leader of an extremely conservative government, has already gone on national television and crisply urged the British public to start using condoms in response to the Aids crisis. It is very hard to imagine President Reagan doing as much. Even if he did—as important as it would be—many Americans would cringe in ways that would be hard for them to explain but that would seem, at least in part, to involve a public figure's presentation of sex as too human, too personally "real."

Meanwhile, we have to proceed; public education is required *now*. What should it be like? If the gay community's hard-won knowledge of Aids prevention has taught us anything, it is that before people can learn to think about Aids, they must be taught to think about the mass of feelings and conflicts comprised in the term *intimacy*. "Particularly for men, whether straight or gay, dealing with Aids means a major revolution in their view of relationships," says Michael Shernoff, a Manhattan psychologist who has conducted dozens of safer sex and Aids-prevention seminars. "We're talking about their ability to sustain intimacy with someone they're sleeping with."

A tall order, perhaps, for a thirty-second educational spot on TV or a condom ad? Not entirely. What media messages about Aids should attempt to do, if they are to succeed, is to create a constructive context for the communication that people will continue between themselves, and to address their concern for each other. But prodding people to seriously consider the subject of Aids does not mean that prevention messages must be pontifically solemn. In England, where, under Mrs. Thatcher's guidance, health officials seem to have actually figured out which sex wears condoms, the BBC invited several ad agencies to submit suggestions for a massive Aids-prevention campaign. One television spot showed a man in bed next to an alluring woman. "What's her name?" inquires a disembodied voice. "I don't know," replies the man, somewhat flustered. The scene changes—the same man, another attractive woman, the same question from the announcer— and the question is repeated with yet another woman. Next, the scene shifts to a doctor's office. "When will there be a cure for Aids?" a voice asks. "I don't know," replies the doctor.

The humor of this ad gave the British, who still have relatively few Aids cases, a sort of national reference point to start talking about the disease; but it still manages to make the point that sex is, preferably, an intimate relationship.

In the United States, where the number of cases has probably eliminated any possibility of humor, a good model for prevention ads may be the AT&T ads for long-distance telephoning. Ads in this mode presents a familiar cultural image of reaching out, caring, and concern for the well-being of others. The American context, moreover, demands advertising that pays attention to all ethnic groups. "I would say that what is needed in TV spots is men from different ethnic groups delivering the same message: 'I'm going to use condoms because I love my woman,' " suggests Michael Shernoff. Whatever the exact words, it is obviously more appealing to ask people to care about another human being than about some terrifying germ they can't even see. Above all, what we do *not* need are more gratingly sincere doomsayers, like those who appear on radio and television at 3 A.M. to tell us that we are going to die from drugs, alcohol, cigarettes, heart disease, and the silent killer, high blood pressure—if somebody else's drunk driving doesn't kill us first.

While media messages can help create a constructive—or destructive—public context for Aids education, much of the basic dialogue about Aids may still take place only on a personal level, in talks between men and women, in discussions among women themselves, and, hopefully, in conversations among men as well. Even to begin that dialogue, it is crucial for men and women to learn about Aids together. This means they must have access to educational seminars where they can learn the ABCs of Aids (how it is transmitted between men and women, how rapidly the epidemic is spreading among heterosexuals, what the situation is in their own community) and where they can discuss some of the tough questions that concern men and women alike. How, for example, should they educate their children about Aids? What should they do if a family member has the disease? The primary intent of basic seminars is not to teach safer sex practices; it is to get both sexes thinking and talking and considering. Bringing men and women together underscores the idea that prevention is a mutual effort involving mutual respect. "If you ever want men and women to talk about their own sexuality together, they must be educated together," insists Claudia

Webster, the Aids Health Educator for the Oregon Health Division.

Good settings for community seminars and educational programs about Aids include churches, businesses, service organizations, health clubs—the new American meeting place—union halls, sports clubs, PTA events, colleges, and meetings of professional societies. Often the best approach is to include Aids education as one subject in a scheduled meeting or program. Many people, worried about Aids, are still reluctant to show their concern. Eddie King, the first Aids educator for the state of Maryland, advises that tenants' meetings at public housing projects are good settings for Aids education. "You just go to the regular meetings. There's always a lot of women there who have questions," he says. "But don't hand out flyers or something like that first, because you'll scare them away before you start."

Materials, pamphlets, videotapes, and films for basic Aids education are now available from a range of sources, including the federal Public Health Service, many local health departments, and local Aids organizations (see Appendix). The American Red Cross, which is currently launching a major education campaign with the Southern Christian Leadership Conference, has informative pamphlets on many aspects of Aids. Its film *Beyond Fear* comes in three twenty-minute segments—"The Virus," "The Individual," and "The Community"—accompanied by lists of suggested questions for audience discussion. Whatever groups or individuals arrange Aids-education programs, it is essential to leave plenty of time for questions, and have somebody there to answer them. Most men and women still have so many specific questions about Aids—ranging from the danger of drinking fountains (none) to the risks of one-night stands (significant)—that they don't focus on the subject of prevention.

However, to voice their own emotions and fears about dealing with men in the shadow of Aids and, above all, to discuss their worries that they may already have been exposed to HIV, women need to be separate.

When a woman fears that she may already have contracted Aids, her best resource, if one is available, would be the small but increasing number of "support groups" for women who know they are at risk or who have a husband or boyfriend who has been diagnosed with Aids. Your local Aids hotline (see Appendix) may have a list of support groups. These groups sometimes meet at hospitals with Aids programs or are sponsored by health departments or local Aids organizations, and they provide immeasurable help and encouragement. Given their embarrassment about asking questions about what wasn't "supposed to be" a woman's disease, many women prefer to ask their first Aids questions on telephone hotlines (see Appendix). Hotlines, of course, are entirely anonymous. "In San Francisco," says Nancy Shaw of the Women's Aids Network, "at least 30 percent of the hotline calls now are from women. The figure has gone up consistently."

Because Aids involves such personal matters, educators are convinced that helping women to confront it involves raising, if not precisely their political consciousness, what might be called their personal consciousness. "Many women just don't want to say anything to a man about Aids because of their fear of being rejected or isolated," explains Dooley Worth, co-leader of a woman's support group at the Stuyvesant Polyclinic on New York's Lower East Side. "So, much of what we try to do is build their self-esteem." In seminars and discussion groups, the technique of role-playing (which means simply having some of the participants spontaneously acting out a possible real-life situation) is often used to express the fears and difficulties of Aids prevention. Afterward, women in the audience are asked to comment on their own reactions to the role-players' situation.

For example, at a daylong conference on women and Aids in New York in late 1986, Sunny Rumsey played a woman who had been out on a few dates with a new boyfriend, and another social worker played the boyfriend. Their dialogue, as passion overtook this make-believe couple at the end of the evening, went something like this:

SHE: I like you very much, but I'd feel uncomfortable without some form of protection. Have you used condoms?

HE: Yes. I used them when I was in the Army. It's no big deal.

SHE: So you wouldn't mind using one?

HE: Well, I don't have any. If I had one I'd use it. So let's go to bed.

SHE: That's okay. If you don't have any, I'll be right back. *(She gets condom.)*

HE: What do you mean? What the hell are you doing walking around with condoms?

SHE: Didn't you just tell me if you had one, you'd use it? Come on, I'll help you put it on.

HE: No way I'm going to put it on! What do you think, I have a disease or something?

SHE: No, I'm not saying you have a disease. I'd just feel more comfortable.

HE: *(Hands her phone number.)* Look, here's my number. When you come to your senses call me. *(He leaves.)*

SHE: *(To audience.)* You know, I like him very much. Maybe I'll give him a few days to calm down and then call him. . . . No! *(Suddenly crumples paper with phone number.)* I have to care for myself more.

The audience discussion afterward addressed such questions as, Can you accept rejection? What are you going to do if he implies you're a tramp for carrying a condom? Would this have worked better if she'd brought up the discussion earlier in the evening? "The aspect that many women seemed to like," Ms. Rumsey relates, "was when she just said, 'I have to care for myself more.' Realistically, they know that some men are going to reject them if they bring up Aids prevention, and they want to be prepared for that."

It is also imperative in Aids discussions to be sensitive to the cultural mores of America's many racial and ethnic groups. "Each culture has its own beat," emphasizes Ms. Rumsey. "In a Spanish Catholic family, if a girl is found carrying a condom in her purse, she can get really branded. If you are dealing with cultures where sexual issues are not discussed at all, you can't expect immediate openness. You have to go slowly. Something like male homosexuality or bisexuality is not mentioned in the black and Hispanic communities. You just don't talk about it. So when women from those communities come in, they are often confronting not only Aids but also the idea that their husband may be involved in a sexual activity they never dreamed was possible."

The great majority of women's organizations, from the Junior League to Hadassah, from NOW to the National Council of Negro Women, provide natural forums for confronting Aids. Moreover, by using such forums, women will start to find their public voice about Aids and their role in Aids policy. Indeed, the almost complete absence of women from Aids policy has been a striking and unsettling feature of the epidemic. To date, only one woman in the United States, Dr. Mathilde Krim, the co-chair of the American Foundation for Aids Research, has been prominently involved in Aids policy. Dr. Barbara Herbert, an organizer for the Women and Aids Project in Washington, D.C., suggests that, ironically, it may be precisely their recent history of activism that has partly deterred women from seriously confronting the issues of Aids. "We've been through so many battles for our autonomy," she says, "that I think many women have looked at Aids and said, 'Oh, no! Why do we have to do it again, and this time against a microbe?' " Whatever the reasons for their absence, women must overcome them.

Obviously, not all women interested in Aids belong to formal organizations, and women do not have to be formally organized to have a helpful discussion. Groups of friends can easily get together to examine the emotions involved in Aids prevention, offer each other support, and discuss such questions as the reactions they are getting from men. A woman could get upset and discouraged by an angry reaction to a condom discussion; but if she hears about the experiences of other women, she may well discover that many men are starting to understand the human values of Aids prevention. One New York bachelor, who concedes that he used to "pretty much follow the male rule that if she didn't sleep with you by the second date, you didn't call her for a third," is now watching his way of life disappear before his eyes. "Women just won't do it," he sighs. "But the truth is, I've started to like having the sexual pressure taken away myself. With it gone, I feel friendlier toward women."

It will be a difficult task to help people discuss and deal effectively with all the tensions, questions, and fears that often stand between women—and men—and Aids prevention. Yet, perhaps the most hopeful sign that prevention, despite the current problems, may start to have a sustained impact in the United States is the atmosphere that has formed around successful community prevention programs. While at first it may seem almost foolish to speak of preventing a fatal venereal disease as a "movement"—in the way that civil rights, feminism, and environmental protection have been "movements"—effective Aids prevention undoubtedly has a similar strength. It is spurred by a committed moral energy that is totally different from life-denying "just say no" slogans, an energy that reaffirms life through the human connection of personal and social responsibility. Hundreds of doctors, nurses, and social workers, as well as Aids patients—homosexuals, addicts, prostitutes, and transfusion victims alike—have already devoted themselves to Aids prevention. They do not judge or censure. Their position is unequivocal: "We don't care who you are, what you did, what's bothering you, how serious your situation is, or how silly your question seems. We're going to stick by you."

And though women have been absent from the public dialogue on Aids, many of them have been on the front lines of real prevention. As counselors, nurses, and social workers, the caring parts of the caring professions, they have talked endlessly to patients, their loved ones, and their families; they have comforted the terrified voices at the other end of hotlines; and they have given help and encouragement to the hesitant women who come to support groups. Before the advertising industry decides to harangue the public about Aids, it would do well to talk to a few of these women, find out how real people feel, and see firsthand not only how terror impedes prevention but also how caring and consideration advance it.

Beyond education, the other major key to public prevention is testing for viral infection. This simple procedure involves drawing about 10 cc (less than half an ounce) of blood from the arm with a needle and syringe. The blood is sent to a laboratory, where it is analyzed for the presence of antibodies produced by the immune system to fight HIV. (In medical terms, people with HIV antibody are said to be seropositive for viral infection.) Since the antibody evidently never wins, doctors presume that seropositive people are also carrying live virus and can transmit it sexually.

Before a woman is told she is seropositive, the blood is

put through a combination of tests that assure a virtually 100 percent-accurate result. Negative tests, however, are sometimes wrong. When blood is tested too soon after infection, the immune system may not have yet produced sufficient antibody for it to be detected. While most infected people produce enough antibody within six weeks, some take six months; a few, up to a year. To reduce the possibility of a false negative result, a woman who believes she has been infected within the past year should have two tests, six months apart. (There are also occasional HIV carriers, including babies infected by their mothers in early pregnancy, who never produce antibody. Yet, they still develop Aids.) The basic lab work for a negative test now costs about ninety cents, for a positive one, about fourteen dollars; and most laboratories can return the results within a few weeks.

Simple as the HIV test is, however, it is a complex social procedure and a harrowing personal experience. Medicine still has little to offer those people who learn they are seropositive, beyond the general advice that healthy living may help and that avoiding further exposures to the virus, whether through sex or drugs, may delay the development of Aids. The HIV test cannot tell *when*—or even *if*—anyone will get Aids. Understandably, for many people, knowledge of seropositivity is terrifying. They wonder, as one woman puts it, "whether every cold or even a tiny pimple is the beginning of the end." For women the blow seems to be especially isolating. Even in many large cities, there are still no support groups for infected women, and the fear of Aids among heterosexuals remains so ferocious that women rarely feel they can turn to those friends or relatives who usually comfort them in a crisis. "This is not a test you can let people just go off and take alone," emphasizes Monnie Callan, a social worker at the Montefiore Medical Center in the Bronx, New York, where one-quarter of all Aids patients are women. "There must be careful counseling before the test and support readily available afterward."

In order to ask people to live with this ominous knowledge, there must be a compelling purpose. That purpose is prevention. In a resounding testament to the human spirit, most people who learn they are seropositive—including homosexuals, hemophiliacs, and drug abusers—even in the wake of their shock, immediately start to change their sex lives by using condoms or safer sex techniques, or by becoming celibate. Indeed, most people who turn out to be virus-free also change their sexual behavior, often by starting to use condoms or being faithful to one partner. It is not surprising that testing has this force even for seronegative individuals. Grateful to have almost literally escaped Aids "this time," they are hardly eager to risk a "next time."

But governments have still not matched this testament by making testing easily available. A few states, including New York, have regulated testing so closely that a test for HIV has been difficult to obtain even from a private doctor. In many states, although tests are available from clinics and private doctors, many people don't want to use these sources because they are afraid the results will appear on their medical records, possibly affecting their health insurance or employment. At alternate sites, by contrast, people do not have to give their name and are reassured that the results will never find their way into their medical records. Because this is the only kind of testing that some people will accept, alternate test sites enormously encourage voluntary testing and responsibility. Yet alternate sites are not widely available, and some areas have none at all. Even with 7,500 cases, and an estimated 500,000 infected people, New York City had only one alternate test site by the end of 1986. (For information on the nearest alternate test site, call your local hotline or health department.)

In some respects, the government's persistent refusal to supply testing has reached the point of cruelty. The experience of AWARE shows that hundreds of women *want* to be tested and be responsible, if only testing were made the least bit comfortable for them. Similarly, when Joseph Lisa, Chairman of the New York City Council Subcommittee on Aids, visited city and state prisons, inmates routinely begged him to arrange for the testing—anonymous or not—that New York prison clinics refused to perform. Without testing, these men were left in the wretched position of not knowing whether they could infect their wives on conjugal visits.

Aside from voluntary testing, public health efforts to fight venereal disease have traditionally involved some mandatory testing. (While testing in venereal disease clinics is not anonymous, in most states it is strictly confidential and clearly should be made confidential in the few states that do not already have strict rules.) For example, most states required all people who went to VD clinics with any infection to be tested for syphilis, even before there was a cure. The purpose—to counsel them about not spreading the disease—is even more important in preventing Aids, since HIV is contagious continuously, whereas the syphilis spirochete has long periods of dormancy during which carriers cannot transmit it. Moreover, men who have had other venereal infections apparently produce a high concentration of T-4 cells—the very cells that HIV preferentially seeks and invade—in their semen, perhaps for the rest of their lives. Given this T-4 overload, these men may be unusually efficient sexual transmitters of Aids.

Also, because people who get "old-fashioned" sexually transmitted diseases are among the first to get a "new" one, venereal disease clinics are perhaps the best places to detect and counsel heterosexuals who have no idea that they are HIV carriers. In early 1985, in research that has never been repeated, the New York City Department of Health found that

3.4 percent of heterosexual, non–drug-abusing men seeking treatment at Manhattan VD clinics for any disease, tested positive for HIV infection. Finally, VD clinics are among the first places where HIV infection can be detected as it enters the teenage population. Preventing the epidemic of HIV among teenagers that we have seen for other sexually transmitted diseases simply has to be a priority. In 1986, the U.S. Public Health Service urged all states to require HIV testing for all patients at their VD clinics; but to date there are no states that have mandatory testing; and in some places, even people who *ask* for an HIV test at a VD clinic still will not be able to get one.

Making HIV testing routine for all hospital patients, as syphilis testing once was, would also make possible enormous gains in prevention, although the problem of confidentiality must be dealt with. By now, studies of both heterosexual and homosexual couples have suggested that sexual transmission of HIV increases as the infected partner starts to get sick. But HIV sometimes attacks in subtle and deceptive ways. At these points, people are often hospitalized briefly, misdiagnosed, and sent home. Only testing can ensure the immediate, correct diagnosis that will alert patients to the need of taking sexual precautions with the person they love. Indeed, the CDC has considered recommending that hospitals, at the least, offer testing to *all* patients, but whether such a recommendation would be followed—any more than the Public Health Service recommendation about testing in VD clinics has been followed—remains to be seen.

"Probably half the patients who come to the medical departments of any hospital have a specific symptom of possible HIV infection, whether it be a low white blood-cell count, fever, weight loss, or neurological signs," says Dr. Craig Wright, Chief of the Infectious Disease Clinic at Walter Reed Medical Center. "As I go around the country, I certainly don't see hospitals testing even half their patients. I don't think we're doing enough here. I'd certainly like to test everybody who comes in. It costs only ninety cents. The idea that experts can somehow pick out infected people without testing is totally wrong. We're experts and we can't pick out everybody. We're following more than four hundred people in various stages of infection and 8 percent of them don't even have swollen lymph glands, which is supposed to be such a classic early symptom. I can also tell you that most of the people we have found early through testing, whether heterosexual or homosexual, were not practicing safer sex or using condoms, so we're glad we got to counsel them when we did."

Other populations that the CDC has considered for testing include pregnant women and people applying for marriage licenses. Dr. Redfield says he would like to see testing so easily available that people could get a test (in this case voluntary) on the way to the movies if they wanted. "Never in public medicine have we had a test whose use has been so restricted," he emphasizes. Indeed, in a bizarre combination of circumstances, the politics that have erupted around Aids have worked to inhibit the life-protecting possibilities of HIV testing. Many liberals concerned with the complex civil-liberties issues, especially confidentiality, that surround Aids testing, oppose any mandatory testing. Indeed, some seropositive people have experienced terrible problems, including losing their jobs and apartments. We cannot allow anyone to be penalized for being tested—it is inhuman and it defeats efforts at prevention. Safeguards and confidentiality are required. "What we need is a federal law," says Dr. Jeffrey Laurence, Director of the Aids Laboratory at New York Hospital, "that blocks even federal agencies from getting the names of those tested."

On the right, fierce hostility toward the major risk groups—homosexuals and drug addicts—has resulted in an equally fierce resistance to all public health measures against the epidemic. Gay health organizations also oppose most, if not all, testing, arguing that since homosexuals appear to be widely following safer sex practices, as witnessed by the plunging rates of venereal disease among gays, there is no point in depressing them with the knowledge they are seropositive. Valid as that argument may be, it is particularly discouraging that these health groups, which have provided such insight into prevention, decline to see or to admit that the general failure to test simply fuels the epidemic.

And women themselves, so experienced in lobbying for public health programs, have been notably uninvolved in Aids policy. Their absence is all the more striking since heterosexual women will probably suffer most from a policy of nontesting. It is they who are being infected by the "occasional" bisexual and the "recreational" drug user who cannot anonymously check their HIV status. It is women who are largely being infected by the men seeking treatment at venereal disease clinics for other infections and who are never tested for HIV. It is women who are largely being infected by men, like New York's prisoners, who have no access to testing.

Yet, politics or not, it is public health officials who are ultimately responsible for the creation of testing policy. In an odd twist of logic, the very fact that women are the new major victims may even be used as an excuse not to test by those officials who have most adamantly refused to encourage—let alone, provide—easy testing. The circumstance that more women than men are now getting HIV heterosexually is used to argue that Aids is still not a *real* heterosexual disease requiring *real* public health measures, probably the first time in medical history that the definition of heterosexual venereal disease has hinged on whether it affects men and women equally. The pages of prominent medical journals are littered with arguments and counterarguments about the relative "efficiency" of HIV transmission from men to women and from women to men. There will not be enough evidence to settle these arguments for years. Indeed, some scientists are still debating the relative efficiency of transmission of syphilis—but that did not stop syphilis testing.

The argument is really about something else: it is about taking full-scale, serious measures to prevent Aids. The few diagnosed cases (so far) among heterosexual men represent about the last, flimsy basis for proclaiming that Aids is a "different" disease, one that doesn't require the public health measures usually taken for venereal diseases. It is appalling that the current vulnerability of women has been exploited to perpetuate policies that are so dangerous to them. This situation serves only to underscore the need for women to become involved in creating public policy.

For a woman, the question of whether or not to be tested is best settled by her own belief that she needs testing. Experience at AWARE and at alternate test sites around the country has shown that women have pretty reliable instincts about when testing is a good idea. Most women ask to be tested because they know or suspect that they've had a sex partner who was at risk, or because they've used drugs. Some women, even though they know of no specific risk but have had several sex partners, just want to be sure they aren't infected. The U.S. Surgeon General has recommended that every sexually active person who has not been in a monogamous relationship during the past five years be tested; some Aids educators suggest that everyone who has not been in a monogamous relationship since 1977, especially those who live in major Aids areas, be tested. There are no hard-and-fast rules. And let's not forget that the great value of HIV testing, aside from prevention, is to end the nightmare of wondering if one is infected. Constant anxiety—not to say terror—is reason enough.

In Connecticut, which has tried to make testing easy by opening eleven alternate test sites, most women come because they have a partner in a risk group, but they also have other reasons. "Several women wanted to be tested just because they'd had numerous sex partners in the past and now want to have a serious relationship or get pregnant," says Jill Strawn, R.N., Aids risk-reduction counselor at the New Haven Department of Health. "Basically, they're looking for a clean bill of health. Fortunately, so far none of the women I've seen in this category has been seropositive. Then, there are cases like one woman who had made out, but had not had intercourse, with a man she later learned was probably bisexual. While she had no risk, she was obsessed with Aids, so I encouraged her to be tested just for her peace of mind. While we do not advise everyone to be tested, we do suggest they get counseling so they can decide if testing is advisable for them."

The most immediate reason that women in all risk categories want testing is to know if it's safe to get pregnant. There is no question that HIV-infected women, even when they appear perfectly healthy, face problematic pregnancies. They can transmit HIV to their babies before birth and probably also by breast-feeding. At least half the prenatally infected babies die before they are two. The strain of pregnancy, moreover, seems to accelerate the disease in mothers, possibly explaining why women generally die faster from Aids than men. About the only ray of hope in this bleak picture is that the rate of maternal transmission may be less than was first thought. Initial research suggested that 65 percent of the babies of HIV-infected mothers are infected at birth. That research, however, was confined to babies born to women who had already had one previous HIV-infected baby. Further study has suggested that some 35 percent of babies born to HIV carriers who haven't had a previously infected child will be infected. If the pregnancy is the mother's first, perhaps 20 percent of babies are infected.

But if the risk to babies may be less than was originally thought, the risk to mothers may be greater. Aids doctors consistently reaffirm their impression that infected women are very likely to first get sick during a pregnancy. And while there are no formal studies, Dr. Wright of Walter Reed, like a growing number of doctors, suspects that even when an infected woman completes a pregnancy without developing serious symptoms, the pregnancy itself will still propel her toward a more acute—and rapidly fatal—disease. "When I sat down to try and figure out why all the diagnosed women we've seen died within twelve months, while some of the men keep going for years, I had to notice that nearly all of the women had been pregnant within the previous two to five years. We know that pregnancy, particularly during the last three months, is a relatively immunosuppressed condition. I very much suspect that the disease process speeds up during that period."

Given the threat to both mother and child, Aids counselors invariably advise women with even the slightest suspicion of risk to get tested before planning a pregnancy and, if they are seropositive, not to get pregnant until much more is known about the combination of pregnancy and Aids. Unfortunately, too often the question of testing doesn't come up until the woman is already pregnant. It is then that a man who has been concealing his own risk may suddenly blurt out the truth, or that a woman's suppressed worries will finally explode and overwhelm her. In a few tragic cases, hospitals and blood banks have had to notify women who were several months pregnant that they were probably infected.

In these cases, more than ever, a woman needs very sympathetic counseling. The possibility of abortion may depend on many factors, including whether she already has children who need her to stay healthy as long as possible. "It is very tough to advise people about pregnancy," comments Denice Deitch, a counselor at the Irwin Memorial Blood Bank in San Francisco. "Some doctors and counselors advise abortion outright. I personally don't. I try to help clarify what the odds are so they can decide. All I can say is, the more I do Aids work, the more amazed I am by the strength that people summon. They somehow get through situations like this."

Whatever the reason for being tested, all women should be aware of certain precautions. Those dependent on private medical insurance should make sure their policies are adequate and paid-for before the test. Women who have a private physician should also request that he not note the test—even when the result is negative—on their regular records. Many people use a false name when they don't have the choice of an alternate test site. Basically, whether they are privately insured or have Medicaid health coverage, most women will do better to seek an alternate site, which not only protects privacy but also usually offers better counseling and information than even the most sympathetic family physicians or gynecologists can give.

The hardest part of testing may well be the two- or three-week period of waiting for the results. During that time, women should remember that, even in a bad situation, the odds of a seronegative result are largely in their favor. To take a worst-case scenario: a woman has realized that her boyfriend is bisexual, and she lives in New York or San Francisco, where the rate of seropositivity among tested homosexuals is 60 to 70 percent. Studies of transmission between homosexuals suggest about a 50 percent chance that her boyfriend could have been infected by his male partner. As we have seen, women have a 20 to 40 percent chance of contracting HIV from a man who doesn't have symptoms. This lowers her real risk from such "double transmission" to about 5 to 15 percent. For a brief relationship, that risk would be even less. For drug-addicted women, the risk varies across the country, from less than 1 percent in New Orleans to 50 percent or more in New York and northern New Jersey.

The kind of counseling that women need after a seropositive result is a very important question. The preventive value of testing consists in making sure that seropositive women, and the men who have infected them or the men *they* infect, understand safer sex. While a special program for women, like AWARE, has had excellent results with safer-sex counseling, some women—especially those without real social supports—may panic and be more easily "lost" to counseling than men, after learning they are seropositive. At some large programs, for example, many women who test seropositive never return for counseling. Part of the problem in large programs may be that doctors (usually men) feel that it is their responsibility to tell women the results—and then refer them to social workers "for further assistance." Yet the doctor, no matter how compassionate, may barely know the woman, and the idea of discussing a sexual—and potentially fatal—disease with a strange man may be so intimidating to many women that they abandon the idea of talking to anyone. "Even if you have a nice doctor in front of you this time, it doesn't make up for the years of bad experiences that women have had with doctors, especially women who use public hospitals and clinics," explains Dr. Herbert. Great consideration should be given to having women be the primary Aids counselors for women.

For women who come for testing because their husband or current boyfriend is seropositive, counseling about sex will be relatively clear-cut. Given the evidence that additional exposures to HIV compromise an endangered immune system, possibly edging people closer to Aids, seropositive couples may be advised to use condoms. A woman tested because of her own risk, whether from drugs or a past sexual relationship, may want considerable help in discussing a seropositive result with her husband or boyfriend. She may need several counseling sessions just to decide how to broach the matter with him, and she may well want to bring her partner for counseling or want the counselor to be there when she tells him.

Women who suspect they were infected by an ex-husband or ex-boyfriend are in a difficult position. For obvious reasons, many people who learn they are seropositive are more than willing to contribute to prevention by making sure that the sex partners on their own "chain of infection" are counseled before the virus can spread further. Still, calling up an "ex" about Aids is hard to do; and for women who just don't know where they contracted HIV, the prospect of dealing with the ex-boyfriends who might have infected them —or whom they may have in turn infected—may be absolutely paralyzing. Contacting people yourself also means letting them know *you* are HIV-infected and losing the privacy that may sustain whatever peace of mind you have left.

Minnesota is apparently the only state where all this has been thought out thoroughly. A seropositive person, while remaining anonymous, can give the Department of Health the names of people to be traced and counseled; or Department of Health counselors will help seropositive individuals to inform their past partners themselves. In the latter case, seropositive individuals rehearse conversations with the counselors before calling or seeing a partner, but the counselors themselves do not have to know the names of the partners being informed. While this program was initiated largely for gay men unwilling to give their partners' names, it certainly can be used by women who want to tell a loved one— even a past loved one—about the possibility of Aids.

However, in the many states where Aids is not treated like a venereal disease that concerns the health department, women will find scant help. Some counselors may be willing to contact partners for them; some counselors may not be allowed to. "This failure to trace and counsel partners is just incomprehensible," states Dr. Wright. "We do it for other diseases that are less dangerous. I mean, here we have health departments every year tracking down thousands and thousands of partners of people who have gonorrhea, and what is gonorrhea compared to Aids?"

Where they can't get assistance, about the only course left to women who want to be responsible, while keeping their own seropositivity private, is to send an anonymous letter. The total refusal of health departments and health officials to help men and women face Aids together will force many people to learn about their HIV status in the worst ways possible: either when they get the mail or when they get sick.

Chapter Five

Drugs, Prostitution, and the Heterosexual Connection

"It is the responsibility of women to look at other women in all walks of life and make sure they are getting the help they need."
—Suki Ports, Minority Task Force on Aids of the Council of Churches of the City of New York

Drugs are a major connection to Aids. At present, 51 percent of the 2,205 women diagnosed since the beginning of the epidemic contracted Aids from drug abuse, and 67 percent of women who contracted it sexually got it from a drug-abusing husband or boyfriend. Moreover, most of the prostitutes who carry the Aids-causing virus are drug abusers. Finally, of the 460 children under thirteen who have the disease, 80 percent have a mother or father—or both—who abused drugs; these children contracted the virus prenatally.

Some 125,000, or 25 percent, of the estimated 500,000 Americans who shoot up drugs are women. The majority are black and Hispanic and live in four states, New York, New Jersey, Florida, and California. Typically, they have a history of physical abuse, and "many have also suffered sexual abuse, often involving incest," emphasizes Deborah Feller, program coordinator at The Door, a social-service agency for adolescents in Manhattan. Most of these women are heroin addicts, though a few inject cocaine.

If it is difficult for outsiders to the world of addiction to understand the compulsion to shoot up at all, it is even harder for most people to understand that a woman would do this. "Sticking a needle in your arm is such an antisocial act," says Edith Springer, a social worker who was herself a heroin addict for ten years. "As stigmatized as addicts are in general, women addicts are totally looked down on. They are rejected by society, their own communities, and their families. There's also an automatic assumption that they're all prostitutes, which is not true."

Counseling addicted women about sexual transmission is no less important than educating addicted men; about 40 percent of non–drug-using husbands of addicted women become infected through sexual intercourse. And both female and male addicts need encouragement to get off drugs or to learn to protect themselves against HIV exposure by properly sterilizing their needles—or not sharing them at all.

The behavior changes among male addicts, especially their concern for their sexual partners, have been an extremely encouraging sign for the overall prospects of controlling the epidemic. As early as 1985, Don Des Jarlais, chief researcher for the New York State Division of Substance Abuse, reported that addicts were widely concerned about reducing Aids risk. "The data clearly contradict the stereotype of intravenous drug users as incapable of modifying their behavior or as unconcerned for their health."

But what applies to male addicts does not necessarily apply to female addicts, whose overwhelming vulnerability and isolation defeat most attempts at routine counseling.

These women are proving to be the risk population that is hardest to reach; they will require very special efforts in prevention.

In the United States, the main focus for stemming Aids among addicts might be described as "needle education," that is, making addicts aware that they should not share needles and teaching them how to sterilize needles if they can't get new ones. (As it happens, New York, New Jersey, and California, which have so many drug-associated Aids cases, are among the few states that require a doctor's prescription to buy a new, sterile needle, so their addicts frequently rely on shared needles.) In some respects, the focus on needle education has occurred by default. Aids has steered addicts toward drug treatment more effectively than anything else, including drug education, drug busts, threats, rejection, and "just say no" slogans. In many states, including New York, New Jersey, California, and Illinois, treatment facilities have been overwhelmed by addicts wanting to give up drugs. But even with their newfound motivation, junkies are not getting the help they seek: space at drug-treatment programs is available for only 20 percent of the nation's addicts.

Nonetheless, even though needle education is second-best to treatment, it can be effective. Even by 1985, eons ago in terms of Aids education, 60 percent of drug addicts in New York City said they were trying to protect themselves from Aids by cleaning their needles or by not sharing them.*

---

*Either rubbing alcohol or diluted household bleach kills HIV rapidly and effectively. To sterilize a needle, pour alcohol, or any chlorine bleach (such as Clorox) diluted with ten parts water, into a small bowl. Draw the solution through the needle until it fills the syringe, and then squirt it out. Next, take apart the needle and syringe, and put the pieces separately into the solution. Let them soak for fifteen minutes. Then rinse all the parts well with tap water. Put the needle and "works" back together, and squirt out any liquid remaining in the needle. "Pull" another rinse of tap water into the syringe through the needle, and squirt it out (thorough rinsing is important to get out any remaining alcohol or bleach). Or

Clearly, given this interest, needle-education programs offer an immediately promising way of preventing the spread of Aids in areas where HIV infection among addicts has not yet reached the levels of New York. The main problem is to *find* addicts and to give them their "lessons."

ADAPT, a group based in Brooklyn, New York, has taken a straightforward approach. Members, who are ex-addicts themselves, go directly into shooting galleries, usually located in abandoned buildings, where junkies are shooting up. They give them lectures and pamphlets about Aids, and literally grab the needles out of their hands to show them then and there how to sterilize them.

Though only people who really know what they're doing should even try these tactics, junkies accept them quite well. A few gallery managers have asked ADAPT for pamphlets and sterilization instructions to hand out themselves. Yet this direct and compassionate effort still does not reach most women; shooting galleries are largely a male world. "The women are back home or out on the streets," says Edith Springer, an ADAPT founder. "To first talk to them, you almost have to approach them one to one. They will never take the first step of coming to you. Just to go to a talk or lecture on Aids, you have to care about yourself, and these women have no self-esteem."

For those women who will come, ADAPT forms small discussion groups. "To get them to care about Aids, we first try to give them a sense of empowerment by putting them with other women who have the same problem. We say, 'Look at us. We used to be drug addicts and now we're not. You can do it too.' Then you have to work with them very personally." Even though they are harder to reach at first, Ms.

---

take apart the needle and syringe, and submerge all parts in rapidly boiling water for fifteen minutes.

Springer feels that women may be more careful about using sterilized needles after they have learned how to sterilize them. "They can keep the needle hidden at home," she adds, "so once they've sterilized it, they don't have to sterilize it again, as long as they don't let anyone else use it." In this very important aspect of Aids prevention, educators who are determined, patient, and willing to invest their own "street time" can break through the daunting isolation of these women.

The unexpected concern of male addicts about preventing the spread of Aids through sex has been profoundly encouraging. In 1985, of 250 addicts interviewed at methadone maintenance-treatment programs or in prisons, 90 percent said they fully understood that HIV acquired through drugs could be transmitted sexually; half said they had already started using condoms, decreased their number of sex partners, or both. Early research shows that the behavior of male addicts (in treatment) who have learned they are seropositive is even more responsible. Among fifteen men in a methadone program in a New York veterans' hospital who were voluntarily tested and told they were seropositive, all immediately started to use condoms or gave up sex until they decided how to deal with their HIV status. Three months later, the two married men had told their wives, and both women wanted to be tested themselves. The steady girlfriends of three men had broken off their relationship; yet, even in romantic disappointment, and the shock of learning they were HIV-infected, only one of the men went back to having sex without using a condom, and only one went back to drugs. And half of the men who tested seronegative also started to use condoms. Many said they just would not press their luck any further or take the risk that the test results could be wrong and that they could unknowingly infect a loved one. "What reaction you'd get from drug abusers still out on the streets I don't know," says Dr. Paul Casadonte, Assistant Chief of Psychiatry at the Veterans Administration Medical Center in Manhattan, "but the care those in treatment have started to take of the health of others is a remarkable comment on the motivation of male drug abusers."

There is, however, reason to fear that this demonstration of responsibility will not easily be repeated by women addicts. The early sexual abuse and violence so common in their experience has left many convinced that they have little, if any, control over sex. "For them, sex is something they're supposed to do for men, not even something pleasurable," says Gretchen Harris, a health educator at the Methadone Maintenance Treatment Center at Bellevue Hospital in Manhattan. "When you talk to them about Aids as a preventable disease and condoms as lifesaving, it's pretty much a foreign concept. Many feel doomed by life anyway and are just waiting for the ax to fall. I feel optimistic that they are changing their needle-sharing behavior, but changing their sexual behavior is going to be a painful, slow process."

To make matters worse, the husbands and boyfriends of these women too often mirror the violent men of their childhood. These men have not generally been counseled about Aids and certainly don't want to hear it from a woman. "So you give a woman a condom," Edith Springer says. "The worst-case scenario is that she goes home and the man kicks her teeth in, which we've had happen. The best-case is that he just refuses to use it. The men in these relationships dictate when, where, and how to have sex. To get them to use condoms we will have to teach the women how to negotiate step by step."

For these women, testing may not be of much use. Regardless of the results, they still cannot do much about men who would rather not listen. Moreover, a positive result may well cut them off from what little social support they do get.

"What has me alarmed," says Ms. Harris, "is that we don't know what most of them are doing after they are tested. We've tested 180, and it's consistently running that 50 percent are seropositive. The physician tells them the results and talks to them. Then they are referred to me for further help, but only about twenty have ever come in. It's very distressing. The rest just seem to go away and lick their wounds at best they can." Aids education for addicted women is very hard to conduct from a large hospital, Ms. Harris has concluded. "I think we have to be out where they are in the community, in housing projects, churches, even laundromats."

Ms. Springer, who is out in the community, has followed four women in drug treatment who learned they were seropositive. "All of them," she relates, "went into a tailspin and went right back to drugs, which meant pills in two cases and shooting up in the other two. Within a few months, three basically did stop their renewed drug use, but the fourth went back to the streets. Since she got another venereal disease, there's no reason to think she was using condoms. Of course, we have to look at every case individually. If you know someone's really out there spreading Aids, you have to try everything. But in general, I don't see that testing these women is doing much good. It's kind of the last straw."

In sum, addicted women are a special population, and the Aids-prevention methods that have worked with other risk groups may not always be effective with them. It is essential to encourage them to sterilize their needles; if they have compassionate support and counseling, some will try to use condoms. But testing should not be recommended without careful, individual evaluation.

Of course, not all women who have used drugs are heavy addicts or currently addicted. For these others, testing may bring relief from constant worry about their HIV status. The longer ago a woman gave up drugs, for example, the less likely she is to be HIV-infected. Women who shot up occasionally, who rarely shared a needle, or who skin-popped instead of injecting into a vein also have less risk. For any woman who ever shot up drugs, the best course is to talk it over with a counselor.

Look for programs in your area that focus on drugs and Aids and, in particular, those like ADAPT which are run by ex-addicts or employ ex-addicts as counselors. (Your local Aids hotline can usually tell you about most of the local programs.) Some programs, like AWARE in San Francisco, are just for women. In the meantime, remember that even though counselors may not advise all women to be tested, they do tell any woman who has ever shot up to take the same precautions against getting—or giving—Aids that she would take if she knew she were infected: never share a needle or donate blood, and make every possible effort to have your sex partner use a condom.

Women married to addicts may also have an interest in testing. When the husband has been diagnosed and the couple is already using safer sex techniques, some women have no wish to know their HIV status (though the majority, in fact, do). But for women who know or suspect their *previous* husband or boyfriend was addicted, testing is crucial to rule out any risk of passing on the virus in another relationship. Without this knowledge, women will never be able to get pregnant without a lurking fear for the safety of their children.

Indeed, even for counselors who don't believe in testing all women addicts, pregnancy is the exception. Because hundreds of Aids-affected babies have already been born to addicted women or wives of addicts, any woman who shot up drugs or whose sex partner was an addict—however briefly—should have an HIV test before planning a pregnancy. The wives of drug addicts—80 percent are not themselves drug-abusers—appear to be widely following this advice. Those who know they are seropositive rarely get pregnant, whether by accident or on purpose; and those who know their husbands are seropositive generally ask to be tested to find out if it is safe for them to have a child. "No one really wants to give Aids to a baby, even if they don't care how they die themselves," says Dr. Cohen.

By contrast, addicted women rarely seek testing or counseling about Aids even before having children. "These are just not women who plan their pregnancies, period—whether around Aids or anything else," says Edith Springer. Whether this will change is very difficult to say although, again, compassion and sustained outreach may have some impact. AWARE, with its community reputation and dedicated street workers, has attracted a number of addicts who wanted to be tested in order to decide about getting pregnant. At Boston's City Hospital, which has a special program of prenatal care for addicted women, some women have started to seek testing before they get pregnant. "The reason the intravenous-drug-user population in Boston sought us out was because they knew we were going to take care of them through a pregnancy," says Dr. Janet Mitchell, formerly Director of Ambulatory Perinatology at Boston City Hospital.

"I think it's very important that the program was set up not around Aids but around the real problem, which is that these were addicted women who needed obstetric care. You don't help them at all to just test and counsel around Aids. It's appalling how programs are increasingly testing for HIV while ignoring the treatment of addiction."

Again, Aids prevention does not occur apart from people's real lives and other problems. All efforts must start from there.

As Aids continues relentlessly on its course, much concern has focused on the role of prostitution in spreading the virus. Potentially, any transmission by prostitution immediately affects several people: the prostitute, the clients, and any other women in the client's life, which often means his wife. Prostitution has been a significant force in spreading Aids in Central African countries like Rwanda, where 80 percent or more of prostitutes are now infected and where condoms are uncommon. In Western countries, for various reasons, prostitution has been less important in spreading Aids. Factors influencing the role of prostitution in Aids transmission include whether prostitutes are drug-addicted, whether Aids has reached a local community, and whether prostitutes are aware of Aids and use condoms or follow safer sex guidelines.

In the United States, rates of infection for streetwalking prostitutes have ranged from 5 percent of those tested in Seattle and 6 percent in Los Angeles, to 19 percent in New York City, and 50 percent in Washington, D.C. In contrast to these women, only one out of twenty $200-an-hour, college-educated call girls tested in Manhattan in early 1986 was seropositive. Drug use partly explains the higher level of infection of street addicts; more than half of those who were seropositive had shot up drugs, as had the one seropositive call girl.

Yet, in focusing on drug use among prostitutes, as many health officials prefer to do, we may be overlooking the importance of sexual transmission in this population. Dr. Margaret Fischl, Director of the Miami Clinical Aids Unit, has pointed out that the 46 percent seropositivity rate for drug-abusing prostitutes in Miami is more than double the 22 percent infection rate for women in Miami who inject drugs but don't engage in prostitution. "A difference like that," she says, "indicates a lot of prostitutes could really have been infected by sexual activity."

Prostitutes are recognized as a significant Aids population worldwide. Infection rates now reported include 49 percent of prostitutes tested in Haiti, 33 percent in Martinique, and 23 percent of drug-abusing prostitutes in Amsterdam. It is very hard to know, however, whether American men who use prostitutes overseas are importing Aids or exporting it. There is little doubt that American military men introduced HIV to the small but growing number of infected prostitutes working near Clark Air Force Base and the Subic Bay Navy Base in the Philippines. Similarly, American tourists (heterosexual as well as homosexual) at least partly introduced HIV to some of the favored vacation areas of the Caribbean, and American soldiers at least partly initiated HIV infection among German and Japanese prostitutes.

Whether a prostitute got HIV from sex or drugs has no bearing on her potential for transmitting it to a man. What may make the difference in Western countries is that prostitutes are increasingly aware of sexual precautions. At the Second International Whores Convention in Brussels, in October 1986, Aids was squarely on the agenda. The 120 prostitutes from sixteen countries issued a resounding call for the use of condoms by prostitutes. In New York City, Dr. Joyce Wallace, an Aids researcher and physician who has widely tested prostitutes, says the use of condoms is almost universal "even for oral sex." As a result, HIV transmission from prostitution may be a diminishing problem in the United States and other Western countries.

But this is notably not true among prostitutes who use drugs. They use condoms so much less that they remain a significant source of potential transmission. The *London Sunday Times,* for instance, has reported that, despite the scorn of other prostitutes, drug-addicted streetwalkers desperate for money will have sex without condoms when men insist. In Miami, condom use among addicted prostitutes is shockingly low; in a group of seropositive prostitutes questioned, most of whom were drug abusers, only 13 percent routinely used condoms.

Still, it is impossible to gauge transmission of HIV by prostitutes in the United States. It has frequently been claimed that, since no individual case of Aids has been traced to a specific prostitute, there probably isn't much transmission. This wishful thinking ignores the fact that no attempt has been made to directly test—let alone trace—customers of prostitutes who are known to be infected, or to trace and test any prostitutes whom men diagnosed with Aids recall as a possible source of infection. All we can say is that, at the end of 1986, the heterosexual Aids-diagnosed men still classified by the CDC as having "no known risk" were asked in a questionnaire if they had used prostitutes; one-third of those who responded said yes. Many had had other venereal infections, typical for men who are promiscuous, use prostitutes, or both.

The situation in Sweden, where Aids epidemiology is taken seriously, is very different. By the time Sweden had some fifty diagnosed cases, at least two were linked to prostitution. One was a heterosexual man, who had almost certainly contracted HIV from a drug-abusing prostitute in Stockholm. The other was a woman who had slept with "Lars," the sailor who became HIV-infected after sleeping with a prostitute in Haiti. Let's look again at the chain of infection that began with Lars. All told, four of the seven Swedish women with whom he slept are infected, as is a boyfriend of one of the women and the son that Lars and his wife had in September 1985. This makes a total (to date) of seven infected people from one prostitute encounter.

No country can ignore the possibility of such a chain of infection, and some European countries have taken various approaches to preventing transmission by prostitutes. Holland has greatly expanded drug-treatment programs for addicted prostitutes (as well as other addicts) and provides free, clean needles as well as safer sex education. The Swedish government, by contrast, now tries to keep drug-addicted prostitutes off the streets entirely, either by repeatedly arresting them or forcibly sending them to drug-treatment centers. (This may be possible because Sweden has only about 150 drug-addicted prostitutes.) It is too soon to know which approach is more effective in curbing HIV infection and transmission. The United States, for its part, seems determined not to provide more treatment or care for addicts, even as punishment. As for prostitutes in particular, there is apparently only one program in the entire country, "Our New Beginnings" in Portland, Oregon, that—because it is staffed by ex-prostitutes—is highly effective in helping prostitutes get off the streets.

Once again, it is the outcast "risk" population that, with virtually no help from public health agencies, has taken most of the initiative in encouraging responsibility. In some cities, the sex industry itself has started to become an important source of Aids prevention and education. At the Chicken Ranch, an internationally known brothel outside of Las Vegas, Nevada, all women are given a monthly HIV test, and customers are required to use condoms. In San Francisco, Coyote, a prostitutes' rights organization, and other groups have steadily organized safer-sex seminars for prostitutes, and progress has even been made with addicted prostitutes. To no one's surprise, the greatest problem for prostitutes trying to take precautions is that heterosexual men are still so badly educated about Aids that *they* don't get the point. "A lot of them argue against condoms," says Gloria Lockett, an ex-prostitute who is co-director of the San Francisco branch of Coyote. "They say, 'But I'm not gay. I can't get that disease.' We've found the best way to deal with them is just to be very matter of fact—like, 'use it, period.' We've thought up a few lines to use. One is, 'Hey, we're in San Francisco.' Another is, 'The fuck is for you and the condom is for your wife.'

"Even addicted prostitutes will try condoms if you make it easy for them," she adds. "One thing I spend a lot of time doing with groups I work with is handing out free condoms, both black and white ones, in the area where addicted prostitutes mostly hang out. It really helps if you put the condom right in their hand. But the addicted ones still give in if the man insists. Why don't men wake up? What can I tell you? To men, a trick is just a trick."

Making prostitution less dangerous in the United States is a difficult task, and no attempt to ban it has ever worked. At present, prostitutes—facing high risk with no help—are the ultimate example of women being expected to halt heterosexual Aids all by themselves. But finally they cannot do it alone; educating the men they deal with must be part of the effort. At the International Aids Conference in Paris in 1986, for example, a doctor from Florida remarked that possibly the most effective Aids prevention message in Miami had been delivered by the anonymous person who spray-painted "AIDS LIVES HERE" in large letters on the metro stop near the red-light district. It is an excellent idea to concentrate on red-light districts, but a better message for the billboards that should go up in every city in the country is, "Heterosexual men *can* get Aids. Use condoms."

Meanwhile, for women who are worried because they suspect their husband or boyfriend has slept with prostitutes, there are several considerations. If he had only oral sex performed on him—and many men who patronize prostitutes do have only that—the risk is minimal. (If we had further studies, we would almost certainly learn that it is nonexistent.) On the other hand, if the man is the kind of bully who wouldn't comply with a prostitute's—or anyone else's—request to use a condom, there would be some reason to worry. While the risks of "double passage"—from prostitute to man to another woman—are small, the example of Lars shows that it can happen. In such cases only a test can give a real answer, and a wife has every right to expect her husband to be tested. The use of prostitutes has, in fact, already become a major reason that heterosexual men cite for seeking voluntary testing. In Japan, where the first woman to die from Aids was a prostitute, the use of prostitutes has become the single leading reason for testing. In the United States, Aids doctors now report receiving steady requests for testing from other doctors who have patronized call girls a few times but don't want to live with any risk that they could unknowingly have become HIV carriers and infect their wives. If a doctor, who can read all the studies showing how small this risk is, finds it mentally insupportable, why should a wife have to live with this question?

Drugs and prostitution pose difficult, rough problems in Aids prevention. We can't solve all of them, and especially with addicted women, progress will be frustratingly slow. Yet the measure of how we can help the most isolated and desperate population affected by Aids is finally a measure of how well we understand the compassion and caring required for Aids prevention in our own lives. Like it or not, these women are a portent for us. For our own sakes, we cannot leave them to wander alone, as so many currently are. "It's a lot of hard work to reach out to them," Dr. Cohen of AWARE concedes. "But whether we do or don't certainly tells us how serious *we* are about Aids prevention, doesn't it?"

Chapter Six

Blood: Giving and Getting

"As yet, there aren't programs to fit the needs of blood recipient cases and their families, and I am not sure we know what their needs really are."—Dr. Shelby Dietrich, Director, Hemophilia Center, Orthopaedic Hospital, Los Angeles

Any disease that affects blood and sex obviously affects two of the most intimate things of life. Blood is perhaps the most symbolically charged component of the body. The word evokes the lifeblood of existence, the bloodlines of family, and the intensity of blood oaths. The idea of blood as bringing death instead of sustaining life is fearsome. Perhaps not surprisingly, surveys show that people worry more about getting Aids from an infected transfusion than from sex. And they continue to worry, even though the risk is now slight: all blood donations in Europe and the United States have been carefully tested for the presence of HIV since mid-1985.

As the traditional guardians of family health, it is largely women who have to contend with the questions and tensions that surround transfusions. What is the risk of the transfusion that I, or my child, had years ago? Should we be tested? Can friends and relatives directly donate blood for my husband? Can I predonate blood for myself? Overwhelmingly, it is wives and mothers who call blood banks to ask these questions. Ironically, they will find a far better definition of the risks to men than to themselves. The good news is that very few women appear to have been infected by blood or blood products, much fewer than men. The bad news is that female blood recipients are the least-studied Aids risk population.

No one has estimates of the seropositivity rates of women who received blood products before 1985. Both logic and evidence from studies of men who received blood products suggest, however, that seropositivity varies enormously according to the frequency of, and medical reasons for, transfusions. Fewer than one in 3,200 women who had simple transfusions may be infected, for example; but as many as 30 percent of those who received clotting-factor concentrate for the treatment of bleeding disorders may be. A woman's interest in testing and counseling would vary as much as these potential risks.

Of the women exposed to HIV through blood products, the group that is probably the smallest in number but highest in rate of infection comprises those with clotting or bleeding disorders. Like hemophiliac men, these women are sometimes treated with clotting-factor concentrate, which is made from the blood of hundreds of donors. But because women's bleeding disorders are usually milder than hemophilia, they need less medical care and fewer injections of concentrate. The chief disorder, von Willebrand's disease (which strikes men and women equally), is sometimes so mild that a woman may not know she has it until some real blow, like a car accident, brings it forcefully to her attention. While it is well accepted that there are 20,000 American men with hemophilia, women with clotting disorders are harder to count, given their intermittent care. "All we can do is estimate from what we see at major hemophilia centers," says Dr. Jonathan Goldsmith, Associate Medical Director of the National Hemophilia Foundation. "About 2 to 3 percent of the patients at treatment centers are women with various factor deficiencies; another 5 to 10 percent have von Willebrand's disease. Then, there will be a few women who are symptomatic carriers of the hemophilia gene." All told, this suggests that some 2,000 women in America are routinely treated for clotting disorders.

Several studies in the United States and Europe have shown that 80 to 90 percent of men with severe hemophilia are seropositive, as are 40 percent of those with moderate hemophilia. Much as these studies have frightened women who use concentrate, there is little doubt that their own situation, while difficult, is less terrifying than that of men. While 267 male hemophiliacs have diagnosed Aids, only seven women with clotting disorders had it as of March 1987. Of course, this figure does not settle the question of the infection rate that underlies the diagnosed patients. The Australians, for example, have reported that 25 percent of von Willebrand's disease patients are seropositive. In the United States, the National Institutes of Health–sponsored transfusion-safety study, the first to massively examine the seropositivity of both men and women who have used concentrate, is still underway. Dr. Natalie Sanders of the Hemophilia Center at Orthopaedic Hospital in Los Angeles reports that in her personal practice only one of three women tested seropositive. Until definitive results are available, the scattered information about women who use concentrate does suggest a seropositivity level below that seen in hemophiliac men.

Given this probable difference, women with clotting disorders may well have different needs for testing and counseling than men. The National Hemophilia Foundation, for example, tells all men with hemophilia simply to assume they are seropositive and take the precaution of using condoms or safer sex practices. Given that there is little chance men will be negative, the foundation does not advise them to be tested unless there is a compelling reason, like research or finding out if it is safe for them to father a child. Almost certainly, however, testing would free more than half of women concentrate users from fear of Aids, no small benefit. If you have a clotting disorder and are unsure about what to do, you will find it helpful to seek counseling to discuss your options and decide which is more important: a chance to be free from fear or the risk of learning that you are seropositive.

Whatever your decision, you should follow the advice given to men about sex: always use condoms or safer sex practices, unless testing has indicated that you are seronegative. There has already been transmission from women with clotting disorders to their male sex partners. "I don't know of published studies," says Dr. James Mosley, Project Director of the Transfusion Safety Study, "but certainly we are now aware of a few instances where the partner of a woman who was infected from concentrate has contracted HIV from her."

Thalassemia is an inherited anemia that affects people of Mediterranean ancestry (chiefly Italian and Greek) and Southeast Asians. In the United States, there are some two thousand transfusion-dependent thalassemics. They usually receive packed red blood cells twice a month. At New York Hospital, which has the nation's largest thalassemia clinic, eleven of the sixty-four transfusion-dependent patients are seropositive; most striking, ten of them are women. "We just don't know why the women predominate like this," says Dr. Margaret Hilgartner, Director of Pediatric Hematology–Oncology at New York Hospital. "At birth, thalassemia divides itself equally between boys and girls. Maybe the women just survive better to adulthood, so there are now more of them to become infected."

These figures from New York may not apply nationally or to other countries. Unlike clotting-factor concentrate, which is manufactured from blood pooled nationwide and even from Europe, packed red blood cells are produced by local blood banks. Even with the multiple transfusions needed by thalassemics, a woman living in a largely Aids-free area would have much less risk of being seropositive. Israel, for example, which has only twenty-five diagnosed Aids patients, has tested 20 percent of its entire thalassemic population and not found anyone, female or male, who was seropositive.

These women may have little incentive to test for HIV. For women with clotting disorders, negative results provide a bridge back to normal life and socializing; except for their concentrate injections and, often, the inadvisability of pregnancy, they can lead active lives. But, for women with a severe anemia who require twice-monthly transfusions, life is restricted no matter what their HIV status. Since they rarely marry, few may need to find out if they are seropositive for the purposes of preventing sexual transmission. (Of course, thalassemic women who do marry or have an affair should use safer sex techniques unless they have tested negative.)

Another problem with testing is that fear, hatred, and misunderstanding of Aids are intense in these women's communities. For a woman from a religious or highly conservative family to learn that she is carrying a virus that supposedly infects only homosexuals and drug addicts can be isolating in the extreme. If you are a thalassemic woman, only you know what even a small chance of learning you are seropositive may mean to you. According to Dr. Hilgartner, those who are positive usually do not even tell their families. "What social support do they get? None!" she says. "I think the only support they may ever get is if we learn to set up programs for them at the hospital."

Sickle-cell anemia, the other major congenital anemia, affects black women and men almost exclusively. Their need for transfusion varies greatly: some sickle-cell patients have no more exposure to blood than other people get through surgery; others require multiple transfusions. About 5 percent of sickle-cell anemics are dependent on routine transfusions, usually about once a month.

In 1985, none of the twenty-six sickle-cell anemia patients tested in New York City who had had routine transfusions was seropositive. However, since then, an ongoing study at Columbia University has suggested that 12 to 15 percent of those with chronic transfusions, women and men alike, may be seropositive. "These are very early numbers, not conclusions," says Dr. Sergio Piomelli, Professor of Pediatrics at Columbia and coordinator of the study. Early results for routinely transfused patients at the University of Miami also show "a small but significant" risk, with no difference between the sexes.

Once again, these results may not hold for relatively Aids-free areas where, unlike New York and Florida, the chances of getting blood from an infected donor did not increase greatly even with numerous transfusions. If you are a sickle-cell patient with a history of multiple transfusions, you would do well to seek expert counseling. "Of course, decisions about testing are very difficult," says Dr. Piomelli. "But our tendency is to recommend it because it protects sex partners."

The largest group who may be worried about past blood exposure are women who received transfusions in the course of surgery before mid-1985. They are indeed an extremely large group, but their risk is minimal. As we have seen, the overall risk of infection from blood transfusion is somewhere in the area of 1 in 3,200; and the risk for women may be even lower.

With their high rate of obstetric and gynecological surgery, women receive 57 percent of the ten million annual transfusions in the United States. However, since these often minor procedures require little blood, women overall receive about the same number of blood units annually as men. Although their Aids risk from transfusion should therefore be equal, only 222 women, compared to 404 men, have so far developed transfusion-induced Aids. Is this because, somehow, fewer transfused women actually got infected? Or did more infected women die from natural causes before they could develop Aids? No one knows.

What we do know is that the low risk does not reassure everyone about past transfusions. If you are sexually active or planning a pregnancy, and you are worried, you have definite reasons to be tested, particularly if your transfusion occurred in a major Aids area. The period of greatest infection from transfusions was 1981 through the spring of 1983, when blood banks first began to warn homosexuals and drug addicts not to donate. In New York and San Francisco, one in 1,000 donors may easily have been infected by then, although no one knows for sure. Other areas had almost no infected donors. Look at your local situation.

In any case, whether you want a test for yourself or are worried about a child or husband who had a transfusion, it is your right to be tested. If your doctor has told you that the risks from transfusion are so low that you are just silly to worry about infection, find another doctor. If you want it, an inexpensive blood test is an entirely reasonable antidote to any concern about Aids. "We have a lot of mothers who call up and ask things like, 'Can you tell me if the donor to my daughter's transfusion in 1980 was okay?' " says Jane Garner, a physician's assistant at the Irwin Memorial Blood Bank in San Francisco. "But we can't know if a donor is infected unless he donated blood again after we started testing. If he was infected in 1985, that doesn't mean he already had HIV in 1980. I highly recommend that a concerned mother take her child for testing, and I particularly recommend that all women in their childbearing years who got a transfusion before mid-1985 be tested themselves."

For a woman who has been notified that a blood bank has traced her transfusion to an infected donor, thorough counseling is essential. Unlike exposures through sex, or even injecting drugs, transfusions are an almost 100 percent-efficient means of transmitting HIV. While very few women received infected blood, nearly all the women who received even one unit will be seropositive. The only buffering factor is that even though the donor now tests positive for HIV infection, he or she might have been virus-free at the time of the donation.

Perhaps because they feel they didn't "do" anything to get HIV, blood recipients are terribly angry and upset when they learn they are seropositive. They also seem to have considerable misunderstandings about viral transmission. "I would say most of my job is explaining how the virus is and is not transmitted," says Denice Deitch, a counselor at Irwin Memorial. "The older transfusion recipients in particular seem to go into a sort of shock; it's as if they're unable to hear what I'm saying. They have real trouble believing that the virus isn't passed on casually. The women are very concerned about whether they can hug their grandchildren. But most of them do want to be tested. They say, 'Well, it's my health, so I better find out.'"

What about today? HIV testing has significantly minimized the danger of infected blood. The major remaining problem is that HIV antibody often doesn't show up in tests for six weeks, and, in some cases, for six months to a year after the virus has entered the body. Refined tests may eventually eliminate this delay, but meanwhile some infected donors are bound to elude testing. "I've seen estimates that maybe a hundred infected donors a year get through," says Dr. Schorr of the American Red Cross, "but the truth is there's no reliable way to estimate the number."

Even though tests that screen blood for HIV antibodies now work so remarkably well, any worry at all about the blood supply is just too much for many people. "It's the mothers who get most upset," says Dr. Charles Pegelow, Interim Director of the University of Miami Sickle Cell Center. "I have one mother who's so frightened, that she won't bring her child in for a necessary transfusion. I think we're getting to the point that some people may not get the care they need."

For those about to undergo surgery, the two major antidotes to anxiety are to predonate one's own blood or to have friends and family donate blood. Some blood banks and hospitals have resisted these practices, but the demands of patients will inevitably oblige them to change. As the epidemic rages, we will have to learn that it is almost as crucial a public health mission to allay unnecessary fear about Aids as it is to encourage constructive concern. Predonating blood is a fine alternative for those who may not need a major amount of blood. Since most people can donate only a unit a week without becoming anemic, the general procedure is to begin about six weeks before surgery, for a maximum of six units, enough to cover most surgical procedures.

And family members and friends with the same blood type can be "designated donors"; in this way, husbands and wives may be able to give to each other or donate blood specifically for their children. (These donors obviously have to be tested first for blood type as well as for Aids and other diseases.) Using designated donors is a bit more complicated than self-donation and has met with even more opposition from blood banks and hospitals. For one thing, extra administrative work is needed to keep track of blood from different sources; for another, family or friends may be no safer than the regular blood-donor population. In fact, in those states where the seropositivity of blood donors has proved to be very low, there is little reason to use designated donors unless it makes you feel better and worry less about yourself or a loved one.

Still, some blood banks, whose numbers will grow, consider designated donors both a safe source of blood and a way to increase the community blood supply. At the pioneering program of the Irwin Memorial Blood Bank, designated donors chosen by family and friends have had an HIV-infection rate of 1 per 1,000, compared with 1.7 per 1,000 for other first-time donors and 3.3 per 1,000 for repeat donors. Over the long term, these are not small differences. The donors chosen by family and friends were generally older or female, groups less likely to have used intravenous drugs or had multiple sex partners, behaviors that increase the risk of HIV infection.

Of course, no one should worry about getting HIV from *donating* blood, because it is impossible. But some *do* worry; fear about donating and the elimination of thousands of risk-group donors have left blood supplies critically low in some areas. Giving blood has become an important public service. You could make that service part of your response to the Aids crisis.

Chapter Seven

What'll We Tell the Kids?

"Sex education is education to respect limits—your own and some-one else's."—Michael Shernoff, psychologist and Aids educator

In California, a father who won a major prize for his first novel, an Academy Award for his second movie, and who generally makes his living with words, decides he must talk to his eighteen-year-old son about Aids.

"Yeah, I know, Dad. I'm supposed to wear a condom," the son replies with the same teenage shrug that has ended parent-child conversations beyond counting.

On Manhattan's Upper East Side, a mother and father come across their five-year-old son and his playmate. Their child, stretched out on the floor, is covered with a blanket.

"What are you doing?" they ask.

"We're playing 'dying from Aids,'" answers the visiting child. Their son, who is playing dead, says nothing. The usually articulate parents are too stunned to comment.

From coast to coast, in small towns, suburbs, and cities,

the question of how and when to talk to children about Aids is looming before parents. No nation has ever faced the challenge of raising children in the face of a fatal, sexually transmitted disease and in a media-saturated society that precludes any chance that the disease can be a topic only for adult concern. As long as Aids lasts, and it may last a very long time, American children will know about it and wonder about what it means almost from the moment they can talk and understand language. "Education about Aids should start in early elementary school and at home so that children can grow up knowing the behavior to avoid to protect themselves from exposure to the Aids virus," Surgeon General C. Everett Koop advised in a major report on Aids in 1986.

But the challenge is not only to ensure that, by the time they start to have their own sexual lives, young people understand the need to protect themselves from Aids. The challenge is to keep an entire generation from coming of age in an atmosphere of pervasive and crippling fear. What about children who play "dying from Aids" at age five? What about a fourteen-year-old girl whose first kiss—one of life's wondrous moments—leads her to worry if she can get Aids that way? (She can't.) "I think children have a lot more questions than parents realize," says Sunny Rumsey. "We have twelve-, thirteen-, and fourteen-year-olds calling up the hotline all the time. Mostly what they want is clear information. They have a lot of misperceptions about how you can or can't get the disease—kissing is a big one—and they're petrified. They welcome the opportunity to have someone sit down and really talk to them."

How to talk to children of different ages may particularly trouble parents. Parents who would find it easy to assure a young child, "You really can't get Aids at all," may find it very disconcerting to talk to a teenager about sexuality. "I don't think that we can expect every parent to turn into a public-health educator," says Sunny Rumsey, "but they can answer questions and listen for what a child of any age is really asking." (Resources for parents and children are listed at the back of the book.)

In its recent pamphlet on discussing Aids with children, SEICUS (Sex Education and Information Council of the United States) advises that the best approach with preschool children is to "set a tone in which children feel free to ask questions about their bodies, health, and sexuality." If the child doesn't seem worried about Aids, or doesn't seem to have paid particular attention to TV or radio reports, there's no point in bringing up the subject. Since asking questions all day about things they have just noticed is a child's main "job" at this age, any fears will probably be expressed fairly quickly.

When a child does bring up Aids, it is what Professor Ronald Moglia, Director of the Human Sexuality Program at New York University and a co-author of the SEICUS pamphlet, calls an "opportunity moment." The child doesn't need a barrage of information, just simple facts that address his worry or question: "Can I get Aids? No. But the baby on TV got it. You can get Aids only when you're a grown-up or before you're born. If you didn't have it when you were a little baby, you won't get it now. Can you get Aids, Mom? I could, but I don't think I will. Daddy and I are very careful, so we won't get it."

Mothers, who are generally most familiar with the questioning streaks of young children, are likely to realize that a child may also be using Aids to ask about something else on his or her mind. Children become gradually aware of death, for example, between the ages of four and eight. "While they're working out a concept of death, their play will focus on whatever they hear about that seems to have a connection with the subject, whether guns, atomic bombs, or Aids," says Dr. Bakeman, Professor of Psychology at Georgia State University. "You can treat this as something for them to play out in their own fashion, or you can get hysterical. Which do you think is better?"

Grade-school children have started to learn that germs and viruses make them sick, and their interest in Aids may center quite specifically on the transmission of disease. A parent can explain that Aids is spread by a virus, but a very different virus from the ones that spread colds and flu. In fact, the parent can say, "It's different from any other virus there is. It's so hard to catch that children can't even catch it, and grown-ups catch it only if they're not careful. But, it's important to know that grown-ups do have to be careful. When they fall in love, they have to take very good care of themselves and the other person." Exactly how much information the parent conveys to pre-teenagers about sexual transmission will depend on what the child already knows about sex. Above all, parents should not end up in the position of giving their first explanation of sex in the middle of discussing Aids. There is no way to say, "I'm going to tell you about a beautiful experience between men and women," in one breath and, in the next breath, "But it could kill you." Remember how astonishing the very idea of sex seemed the first time it really struck you, and imagine how shattering it would have been to get a message about a fatal disease at the same moment.

By the time children are thirteen, they are in dangerous territory if they don't specifically understand that Aids is transmitted by vaginal and anal intercourse as well as by injecting drugs with an infected needle. There's no way to speak about these subjects except directly and bluntly. Euphemisms, such as people get it from "going to bed together," are only confusing. Parents must be sure that children truly understand that anybody can get Aids from sexual intercourse; they must remember that their children have now heard five years of the false message that Aids is a disease of homosexuals. "The boys start with a macho attitude," says Alan Marshall, a special counselor at Junior High School 229 in the Bronx. "Their idea is 'so long as I'm not messing with a homo, I'm not going to get it.' For the girls, it's a real mystery. 'How can I get it if I'm not a man? I'm never going to get it.' " Many teenagers also do not realize that someone who actually got the virus from drugs can then transmit it sexually.

Just explaining the basics—vaginal and anal intercourse and injecting drugs—will make many parents very uncomfortable. "Lots of parents tell me, 'I don't know what to say,' " relates Eddie King, the first Aids educator for the state of Maryland. "But it turns out that of course they do know what to say. They just never thought they'd have to use these words to their kids. I advise them to do some reading about Aids before they start—get to know the subject—and then just psych themselves up and be very blunt." Whether parents wish to proceed beyond these indispensable basics to a thorough discussion of prevention will depend on their own views and sense of comfort or discomfort. Parents who don't picture themselves talking about safer sex practices with their children, or explaining condoms even to older teenagers, should not do so. Even if a parent just directs teenagers to a hotline number, where they can ask questions, or gives them a book or pamphlet, this can be enough to help them understand that there are places to find out about Aids.

However, this is hardly to suggest that the parents' role stops with providing information. The facts are only the beginning; for children as much as for adults, education in values is the core of Aids education. Since kids don't understand sex very well, it is particularly hard for them to understand how deeply it involves responsibility for themselves and for others. "There's no substitute for the parent as the primary sex educator of values," emphasizes Dr. Sol Gordon, author of *How to Raise a Child Conservatively in a Permissive World.* "You have to talk to your children about values, whether you're comfortable talking about sex or not."

Indeed, if Aids education is to succeed at all, it must be instilled with values that are far more appealing—and appealing to the true idealism of teenagers—than has been the case for sex education to date. Sex education in the United States is barely tolerated, and tolerated grudgingly for a single message, "Don't get pregnant." As the one million annual teen pregnancies in America tell us, this one-note theme has failed completely. Applied to Aids, it will also fail. "The one message of 'No, just don't have sex,' is bankrupt," says Dr. Gordon. "We all know that it is totally hypocritical. Fewer than 10 percent of American couples are both virgins on their wedding night. Parents should send the other message too: 'If you have sex, be responsible.' "

Using Aids to threaten kids is disastrous. Not only is it just plain mean to menace a child's sexual identity by bellowing, "Do what I say or you'll die from Aids!" but the challenge of danger can be an aphrodisiac for teenagers. While the actuality of death is very remote, the idea of taking a major risk for love is immediately enticing; it is part of their idealism. Shakespeare had good reason to make Romeo and Juliet fifteen and thirteen. On the other hand, speaking to the heroic, as distinct from the reckless, in teenagers' idealism can be a very powerful force for sexual responsibility. The truth of Aids, which doesn't have to be varnished or exaggerated in any way, is that an individual's moral stance has a direct impact on life and death in his or her world. By being sexually responsible, teenagers are being special and outstanding, and are contributing to the welfare of their friends and community.

Even though Aids can be a hugely uncomfortable subject, parents may ultimately find that it initiates family discussions about values and personal responsibility that would otherwise never have occurred. Try to listen for what a teenager is asking. Group pressures are so strong that much of what teenagers may really be asking is how they can be responsible and to be one of the gang at the same time. This group behavior is particularly potent in the sexual behavior of boys. "A main point of our message," says Dr. Richard Keeling, head of the American College Health Education Task Force on Aids, "is to teach young men that when a girl says no she means it, and that when she says use a condom she means it." Here is an opportunity to encourage your child's growth in personal values: "I know you've always had a strong concern for other people, and you don't want to act in any way that could ever harm others, no matter what your friends are doing."

A good way to have good Aids conversations at home would be to start having good Aids information in the schools. Parents should be very interested in seeing that their children's schools start to teach about Aids and should support educators trying to initiate programs. "The more articulate and influential parents will just have to demand that the schools educate about Aids and demand that all children be educated in the language they best understand, whether it's Spanish or Swahili," says Suki Ports, director of the Minority Task Force on Aids of the Council of Churches of New York City.

Although there are not yet many materials for younger children, there are now enough high-school materials so that schools everywhere and of all types—public, private, parochial—should be able to find some acceptable approach to teach about Aids in the classroom. Resources range, for example, from a simple, three-session course on Aids transmission and prevention, developed by the Oregon State Health Division, to the very forceful and graphic videotape, "Sex, Drugs, and Aids," produced for the New York City Board of Education. "Teaching Aids," a high-school course produced by Network Publications in Santa Cruz, California, is particularly thorough and interesting about the physiology of Aids, including how viruses work and what past epidemics show us, a strong point for today's technologically sophisticated children.

School systems not ready to offer thorough Aids education in the classroom can have "Aids Evenings" sponsored either by the school or by the PTA, for both children and parents. For single mothers, who often serve as the sole source of guidance and admonition on so many subjects, school programs about Aids may be doubly important as a backup. Michael Shernoff suggests that the evening hour is best for school-sponsored Aids discussions, so that working parents of both sexes can attend. The point of these evenings, beyond conveying basic information about Aids, is to get parents and children talking. Mr. Shernoff suggests beginning with a brief lecture on the facts—"Aids 101," as he puts it—allowing time afterward for questions and then breaking up the audience into groups of three or four families, each with a counselor or teacher leading the discussion.

In these smaller groups, the focus is on what parents want children to know about responsible sexual behavior and what children really want to know from parents about Aids. As always, role-playing scenarios are a good way to start a discussion, and role playing that is exaggerated or that shows human shortcomings gets the audience to think about more effective approaches. In one possible scenario, for instance, a father walks in on his daughter, ensconced on the couch and necking with her boyfriend. A son and daughter from another family should play the teenager pair, to free the acting and dialogue; and the father might be encouraged to act angry, even if he wouldn't be in real life.

FATHER: What are you doing?
CINDY: Well, we're . . .
BOBBY: Hi, Mr. Smith.

FATHER: You are to leave right now. Get going.

BOBBY: Well, so long.

CINDY: 'Bye, Bobby.

FATHER: I asked you what you were doing.

CINDY: Just sitting.

FATHER: No, you weren't.

CINDY: Yes, we were.

FATHER: Haven't you heard of Aids?

CINDY: So what?

FATHER: So *what?* How stupid are you? Do you want to get killed or what?

CINDY: What do I care?

FATHER: You'd better care!

CINDY: I'm going to my room.

This scene might give rise to a discussion of the following questions: Is this father really concerned about Aids, or is his daughter's sexual behavior his main worry? Could his daughter have changed the course of the discussion, for example, by asking how you really get Aids? If the father wanted to talk about Aids, should he have asked Bobby to stay so that both young people would learn from the discussion? Would the father have acted differently if his child were a son?

The question of whether there are separate issues in talking to sons and daughters often comes up in Aids evenings. According to a number of Aids educators, parents generally seem to find it easier to talk to their sons about Aids than to their daughters. "They pretty much expect boys to be sexual, so they unconsciously feel it's all right to talk to them about sex," says Mr. King. "With the daughters, they want to be gentler, less blunt. I am much more often asked by mothers how to talk about Aids to a daughter than to a son."

While education about Aids transmission is just as important for girls as for boys, parents must realize that sexual pressures are different for each gender. For girls, according to

Susan Newcomer, Director of Education for the Planned Parenthood Federation of America, a major question is simply how to say no nicely—or say no and still be liked. "It helps girls to discuss the specific replies they can give a boy, whether it be that sex isn't a test of love, or that they're not ready, or that they're scared, or simply that they don't have to if they don't want to. From time to time, ask them what boys say to them," she suggests, "and what they think about what boys say to them."

Boys' enormous sense of invulnerability, the entrenched male teenage myth that they can't get hurt and that even if they do they certainly won't die, is perhaps their major block to acknowledging that Aids is a real danger. The long incubation period between infection and disease makes it unlikely that many teenagers will be forced to face a friend's illness and death. Mr. King suggests trying to pierce this sense of invulnerability by employing very specific facts and statistics about Aids. "Tell them that for every diagnosed case, doctors estimate that there are another fifty to one hundred people infected with the virus," he says. "And don't give them the same old sexually transmitted disease lecture. They've heard it already. Make sure they understand how Aids is different: that they won't get the itching or sores they would with herpes or gonorrhea. And that they can't go and get a quick shot of penicillin and be back in the running a few weeks later."

The other obstacle for teenage boys in understanding Aids is that they can be so anxious about their own sexual identity that they don't want to discuss homosexual behavior at all. It is very important, however, that parents be explicit in explaining that anal sex is a very risky behavior. Using phrases like "homosexual experience" is confusing; to a worried adolescent, that could easily imply that standing around in the locker room masturbating with his friends has exposed him to mortal danger. Once again, be simple but clear.

Parents should remember that Aids education is not only for today or tomorrow but that it will loom as a responsibility for years to come. That is why it is crucial, even while being blunt, not to overwhelm children with doom and gloom. After a while, they just won't pay attention, and "after a while" is likely to be when they're older and closer to being sexually involved. "You don't want to close the door," says Sunny Rumsey. "Many times, a kid will ask for information and get a twenty-minute lecture instead. A child who gets a hard time won't come back again." It is better if parents bring up the subject of Aids in an interested but conversational way from time to time, simply by asking questions of their own: "Oh, what do the kids in school think about Aids? Do they ever discuss it? Do you agree with what they say?"

Sadly, Aids counselors see little sign that parents are aware of the crisis that Aids represents. Alan Marshall, for example, says that in all his counseling sessions with the parents of junior high school students, no parent has yet raised the subject. Similarly, Dr. Nat Floyd, a psychologist who works with troubled teenage boys in Westchester County, a suburban enclave outside New York City, says that not one parent has asked him about Aids. On the contrary, the "Aids outlook" that many of these children pick up in their communities has blinded them. "Among suburban adolescents," he explains, "there's a lot of scapegoating. Aids gives them somebody to look down on. The groups that the disease struck first, homosexuals and drug addicts, are so stigmatized by these kids—an attitude they often learn from their parents—that, as far as they're concerned, Aids is happening in outer space."

The price to pay for letting children think they are immune, that Aids travels by groups rather than by individual behavior, will become higher and higher. While we do not know how much HIV infection has reached high schools and colleges, doctors who have diagnosed students either with infection or with early symptoms of Aids itself are staggered by their continuing misperceptions about how the disease is transmitted. A major Aids doctor in the South recently saw a nineteen-year-old college girl whose HIV infection was confirmed after she sought treatment for persistently swollen lymph nodes. "The tragedy was that she evidently knew her boyfriend was bisexual and that there were a couple of boys in her group who had pretty much openly said they were bisexual," the physician says. "Yet none of them seemed to have any concept of the danger."

In a similar case at a college in Virginia, a young woman became infected after having a three-week affair with a male student who had spent two nights with a male friend. "The boy who transmitted the virus to the girl would never have defined himself as bisexual," Dr. Keeling emphasizes. "That's typical of how a straight kid thinks. If it happened only once or twice and he's not gay, he's not in a risk group." Dr. Keeling urges colleges to actively educate students about the real risks for Aids, by thoroughly explaining the idea of "risky behavior" as opposed to the fallacy that the virus is confined to "risk groups." He also thinks colleges should offer easily available testing or testing referrals for students who have any reason at all to think they may have been infected.

Let's be fair. What kids now face is not easy. We have never had to convey such serious information about sex so widely to people coming of age sexually. Aids is the first 100 percent–fatal sexual disease ever known. In the end, in the face of that dismal fact, the momentous challenge for parents will be not just to convey information and values but also to protect the sense of wonder about sex. Always the accompanying message should be, "I am telling you this because I love you and never want you to get sick from something as wonderful as sex."

Chapter Eight

After a Diagnosis

"I guess if there's one thing I'd like women to understand, it's that you can go on, just living your life, day by day."—Simone, seropositive woman

In the year after she realized her swollen lymph nodes were a symptom of HIV infection, Simone embarked on what she calls "a search for sanity." Even though most of her energy and concern was focused on her husband, who was dying from Aids caused by the drug habit he had given up eight years previously, Simone also had to face the significance of her own seropositivity. "I kept thinking over and over, 'What's the worst that could happen?' It may seem like such an obvious answer, but it took me a year to figure out: 'The worst that could happen is that I'll die.' Once I said that to myself, I could function. I mean, I could die today anyway—I could get hit by a truck.

"I began to do practical things," Simone recalls. "I went to the Gay Men's Health Crisis, and they helped me make a living will, which has instructions for how much medical care you really want. Strange as it may seem, that made me feel better. I felt like I was taking some control over the situation. Of course, I still have terrible panic attacks, but I can now go for weeks and not even think about it. Whatever life I have left, I just want to live it. There's nowhere to run anyway."

By now, hundreds of women in the United States and, increasingly, in other countries know they are seropositive but have no symptoms of illness or, like Simone, have only minor symptoms that don't interfere with normal activities. We have no idea how many of these women will get Aids, but most of them will certainly live for years. In groups of homosexuals studied, for example, 70 percent of those with the early symptom of lymphadenopathy still had not developed Aids after five years; and while large groups of women have not yet been similarly monitored, some have been infected for six years without developing symptoms.

The growing knowledge about helping seropositive people suggests that quite possibly—although, again, there are no studies—some measures may help prolong life. The Community Health Project, a Manhattan clinic associated with Bellevue Hospital, recommends the following: "We advise a good diet and plenty of rest, and that you keep exercising as you've been accustomed to. If you usually go to the gym a couple of times a week, you don't have to stop just because you are seropositive," says Denise Ribble, R.N., health educator at the Project. "Of course, you should try to avoid getting any infection, like a cold or the flu, that puts a strain on the immune system. We recommend having flu shots, because the shot is less of a strain than the flu itself. But you shouldn't have any live vaccines, a category that includes vaccination for measles and smallpox."

Seropositive women should also avoid any additional exposures to HIV, whether from sex or drugs. These exposures almost certainly kill T-4 lymphocytes, further compromising the immune system. Sperm itself, whether infected or not, may also be a strain on the immune system because it is a "foreign protein" that provokes mild, allergic reactions in some women. Condoms and safer sex practices therefore are doubly important. "Avoiding immunological stress also means that women with allergies should be very careful to keep away from the foods or substances they already know bother them," adds Ms. Ribble. Aside from these general guidelines, seropositive women may need little medical attention. At the Community Health Project, asymptomatic women come for a checkup only once every six months, a schedule that seems to have become fairly standard.

For seropositive people, not knowing when they could get sick is perhaps the worst aspect of being infected, and it makes living with the virus rather like living with a nasty fortune-teller who knows the future but won't tell. At outpatient centers for seropositive individuals, alleviating this emotional toll is a primary aim. "People can pray, chant, do yoga, get counseling, or go to support groups. We don't care what it is," says Ms. Ribble, "but they need to to deal with the stress of worrying all the time whether they're going to get ill. That stress in itself may accelerate the disease. On the other hand, we now believe that people who take control over their condition truly do stay well longer."

In searching for control, seropositive women would certainly benefit from the warmth and reassurance of support groups. Some formal groups are now available. In San Francisco there is even a phone support group for women who live out of the city. But on the whole, support groups exclusively for seropositive women are still hard to find. While women are usually welcome in gay groups, the emotions involved in being seropositive are so primary to sex that groups mixed by gender or sexual orientation just don't work as well.

The problem for seropositive women is twofold. They lack the organizations, like those for gay men, that have tirelessly addressed the emotional turmoil of being infected with HIV, and many women still feel so stigmatized that they do not try to get help for their pain. Simone, for example, is now trying to organize a support group in the Bronx, a New York City borough with more than two hundred women with diagnosed Aids and hundreds more who are seropositive. "I'm sure once we get started, a lot of people will come in. They need it," she says. "But what you have to understand is that women who have this disease are just so ashamed that they stay in the house and hide even when they're not sick. I couldn't do it that way myself. I was in too much pain not to get help, so I went to some meetings of gay support groups. Somebody had to tell me that feeling as crazy as I did about this at first was normal. Then I felt better."

There are other ways for women to begin taking control of their lives. Drawing up a will ensures that your property and possessions will be distributed as you would want. Rather than being depressing, it can be a relief to give this kind of direction to the future. Many women may also find relief, as Simone did, in drawing up a living will, which gives instructions for medical care, should they become incapacitated or incompetent. The legal force of living wills varies from state to state, but they are probably the best available way to try to enforce your wishes if, for example, you don't want to be put on a respirator or have other heroic measures taken to keep you alive.

Finances usually present a major challenge. Working women who feel well usually want to keep their job, for the sense of normalcy it provides, as well as for the income. Women who have to stop working because they feel tired (but do not necessarily have any of those opportunistic infections which signal the onset of Aids) may find the best financial help in Supplemental Security Income (commonly known as SSI), a program of the Social Security Administration. SSI provides income for the disabled or chronically ill without resources. And, since you do not have to be previously employed to be eligible, social workers widely advise seropositive women on welfare to switch to SSI when they become medically eligible. "You don't get all the hassles you get from welfare departments. With welfare, when you're sick and can't keep your appointments, they often try to take you off," explains Edith Springer of ADAPT. "But since SSI is made for people who are sick, there isn't the same problem. The only real problem with SSI has been a regulation that people who are in the hospital for a month are supposed to get only $25 for that month. However, they're now more willing to negotiate over that. They've realized this means people can't pay their rent and that there are even more problems if they get kicked out on the street."

At this point, the most helpful person in a seropositive woman's life will probably not be her doctor but a sympathetic social worker. Social workers who specialize in helping HIV-infected people, whether inpatients or outpatients, can be found at most major hospitals with Aids centers. Gay organizations and other community groups also have advisers who help people figure out the often complex requirements for obtaining welfare, Medicaid, and Social Security. Use these advisers and social workers. Dealing with social welfare agencies yourself can be very daunting, not to say stressful, especially if you have never done so. "Thank goodness I have a helpful social worker," says a Florida woman who wants to be known only as Mary. "I worked my whole life and I never had to do this. For me, getting financial assistance has been the most embarrassing and upsetting part of my condition. I can't understand the regulations. You are told many different things. First I was on Medicaid, then I was taken off. I still don't know why."

Unfortunately, just when she needs it most, a woman may find herself cut off from that most feminine source of solace, intimate health talks with girlfriends, sisters, mothers, and other women. Many women prefer not to tell their usual confidantes that they are seropositive. "This is not the sort of thing women want to talk about with their sister or even their family doctor, that is, all the people women are used to talking to about health problems," Dr. Cohen explains. "Even those who got the disease from a transfusion feel they are stigmatized and that somehow they have to prove they haven't done something bad."

But if you can truly confide in a friend or close relative, it will certainly help. Seropositivity is a heavy burden to carry alone. Women who are married or living with a man, and who contracted HIV not from him but from a transfusion, drugs, or even a past relationship, may find their partner the hardest person to tell. Married women often want a social worker, doctor, or nurse to help explain the virus to their husband. In this way, they feel, he will understand the sexual precautions better and be fully reassured that the disease isn't transmitted casually.

The question of talking to children is often paramount. Most women, even if they tell no one else, feel it is best to tell the children almost right away. Frequently, a husband or father is already sick, so there is no way to hide the facts. But, more than that, children have uncanny ways of sensing their mom is upset. To some extent, a mother's explanation will depend on the child's age. To young children, she can simply say that, if she seems sad and depressed, it's because she learned she has a virus that isn't making her sick now but possibly could make her sick in a few years. Mothers will get a lot of sympathy from children, but they should also be prepared for anger, especially from those old enough to understand that the virus is sexually transmitted. "My oldest son was furious for a year," Simone says, "which is part of the reason I'm glad we worked it out now. It took us that long, conversation after conversation. I just had to keep explaining it was nobody's fault. My husband didn't know and I didn't know. There was nothing we could have done to prevent it at the time."

However, because of fear that children will be shunned or taunted, mothers generally consider it best to advise them not to tell their own friends. "You can say your mother is sick, but just say she has cancer," Mary told her children. "From what I've seen, there's so much fear and misunderstanding about this disease that I don't think it would help them if it became known I had it." Simone sent her children for counseling, not only as an outlet for their anger but also so they would thoroughly understand that they couldn't contract the virus from her. And for many mothers, total reassurance that the children will be all right is critical. In their first dread, they may simply not believe that the virus is transmitted to a child only during pregnancy and that her older children are bound to be virus-free. "If a mother's worried at all, I suggest just testing the whole family," says Jane Garner of the Irwin Memorial Blood Bank. "I cannot tell you what a relief it is for seropositive women to have proof that the children are fine."

Although many seropositive women have learned to live constructively and calmly, their lives change rapidly if they are diagnosed with Aids. Particularly for women who didn't know they were seropositive, and never had time to prepare their families, a sudden or unexpected diagnosis can throw them and their children into turmoil. "These women need a lot of information and help," says Monnie Callan, a social worker who counsels many heterosexuals with Aids. "And they need it quickly." The amount of time that women live after diagnosis of an Aids-related opportunistic infection varies from several weeks to two years; however, most women die within the first year.

At present, the only medical treatment that has been shown to significantly lengthen life is azidothymidine (AZT). Daily doses of AZT pills have so far been prescribed almost exclusively for patients who have survived one attack of pneumocystis pneumonia. In research trials, only 2 of the 145 patients on AZT had died after four to seven months, compared with 22 deaths among 137 patients taking a placebo. While 13 women—6 on AZT and 7 taking a placebo—were included in these trials, no separate information about the female survival rate is available. It is also unknown whether women are more likely to get the severe anemia that is a side effect for about 30 percent of patients on AZT and that often necessitates routine transfusions. All told, AZT is an important step in prolonging life, but since it does not kill all virus in the body, it is not a cure. The women on AZT, although glad to get the drug, still continue to face the essential problems of being an Aids patient.

Priscilla Diaz sat in a wheelchair at the Bronx Municipal Hospital Center in New York. She was thirty-seven years old and weighed ninety pounds. She had contracted Aids from her husband, a drug abuser whom she had left four years earlier and who had died from the disease. On her lap were two very womanly possessions—her make-up bag and a large envelope containing dozens of pictures of her four children—charged symbols for the woman with Aids.

Priscilla Diaz's children—five-year-old twin boys, a seven-year-old girl, and a sixteen-year-old son—had been sent to live with relatives outside New York, and she was alone. Priscilla's oldest son had wanted to stay to assist her, but she felt that would have been an unfair burden. She missed her children terribly, and phone conversations with them were the highlight of her life.

She also missed what might be called the frivolously profound joys of being a woman. All those concerns of clothes and make-up are particularly assaulted by a wasting disease like Aids, which often ravages one's appearance as it attacks the body. Priscilla painted her nails bright pink, and even while she had to wear smaller and smaller clothes, down to children's sizes, she kept wearing pretty, bright outfits. With no assistance from day to day, however, keeping her appearance took concentrated energy. Family members and friends occasionally dropped by, but fear of Aids kept most people away.

Priscilla, however, was fortunate to find a hospital with a well-developed Aids program where people knew how to help her with the legal and practical matters that become urgent. Some hospitals that treat Aids patients now have staff lawyers to help with legal needs like wills for property and living wills; and local Aids organizations can often recommend volunteer or low-cost lawyers.

But the greatest challenge in a woman's personal affairs is almost always how to settle the custody of her children. Fearing that assigning them to family members could provoke quarrels or draw too much attention to their condition, even women who knew they were seropositive may have held off arranging custody; but with the diagnosis of Aids it is imperative. "If a mother doesn't complete her arrangements," emphasizes Monnie Callan, "the children can end up in a terrible limbo." Sometimes these arrangements are easily made, but a woman should not be surprised if all the tensions over her disease, plus simmering family quarrels, in-law jealousy, and other family differences, erupt over the custody of children. The problem is often not that the children have no place to go but that there are conflicting claims for them. In trying to decide what is best, a woman may well want to ask other family members to meet with her social worker so that the family can concentrate on the children without getting sidetracked by other problems.

Even aside from settling child custody, the first few months after a diagnosis of Aids can be marked by severe family tensions and anger. Aids easily serves as a catalyst for old family quarrels and conflicts, particularly when it has been sexually transmitted. "Battles that have been there can come up forcefully," says Monnie Callan. "Parents will say things like, 'I told you not to marry him, and now look!' Remember that a husband is often already dead, so the family is at a breaking point. It's a very stressful disease."

A woman's mother may be the one who gets most upset. "I'm not sure why, but mothers seem to adjust better when sons are diagnosed, no matter how they acquired the disease," observes Marge Fenn, coordinating nurse in the Aids program of Bronx Municipal Hospital. "Mothers and daughters will often be at terrible odds at first, no matter how much education and social work there's been. I suspect this may be because the mothers identify with the daughters—'here is another woman who has been hurt or victimized.' The daughter will just have to be aware that her mother will bridge the gap and come around. They almost always do. After all, this is their child." Indeed, after the first months of tension, almost everyone in families does "come around." As social workers observe, the family members from whom a woman expected the least help will often extend her the greatest support.

Even after custody is arranged, children should remain with the mother for as long as she feels able to care for them. At the present time, because of Medicare and insurance restrictions on home health care, women often have to fight to get the assistance that would enable them to keep their children longer. But this situation is bound to change. As Dr. Carol Harris of Bronx Municipal Hospital puts it, "Insurers and public health officials will simply have to start seeing Aids as a family illness."

After the mother is too sick to have the children stay with

her, they should still visit—often. A continuing involvement with the mother, although not necessarily with her medical procedures, is the best thing for both mother and child. It makes the mother happy, and it may ease the children's trauma. To be sent away and told months later that their mother has died can make children worry that their leaving was connected to her death and that, somehow, if they had been there, she would have lived.

Just before Priscilla Diaz's final hospitalization, her children came back to be with her. The importance of this last visit was clear. Her daughter told relatives she was "going to help mommy by cleaning the house"; for her oldest son, it was a time of great closeness with his mother. It is hard not to believe that children who have had the chance to say goodbye in their own way—and "help mommy" in their own way—won't be better off. Yet, given the stigma of this disease, we must realize that even with sensitive attention from family and friends, and all that a mother does to protect and help her children, "many need counseling for months or years," says Monnie Callan.

Dignity, of course, matters until the minute life ends. Isolated and fearful as women feel when they are first diagnosed, the worst fear of many is that they will never again have the repose of dignity. But those who care for Aids patients—doctors, nurses, and family alike—say again and again that these women and men somehow attain a remarkable peace and faith. It is as if they finally draw both uncommon strength and understanding from their struggles with this uncommon tragedy.

"I never expected anything like this to happen to me," Priscilla Diaz stated calmly but forcefully, "but it did. I accept it. I can still feel happy. Whenever I'm well enough, I still go out. You've got to have faith. Deep, deep faith."

Chapter Nine

The Caring Woman

"I can only say I love him."—Mother of son with Aids

When Aids afflicts a family, no matter whether the patient is a son, daughter, husband, in-law, or cousin, women often find that the stress of the disease is somehow shifted onto them. "This is the 'rippling effect' of Aids for women," says Sunny Rumsey. "They end up in the middle of the battlefield. You have a mother who will defend a child against a husband, or a grandmother trying to soothe everyone. Sometimes the person with Aids can be very angry, and the woman has to cope with that. These women don't get much support." If a husband is the patient, the woman may find herself particularly alone. When men feel they might have infected a wife or girlfriend, they may find their own illness almost impossible to discuss; and the silence compounds the wife's stress. The National Hemophilia Foundation, for example, has found that few hemophiliac men with Aids will go to therapy or support groups; they can hardly talk about the situation to anyone.

"They just feel so guilty," explains Peggy Heine, M.S.W., an Aids specialist with the foundation. "What we have found is that the wives are more and more asking for support groups."

Although the advice to find a support group may have begun to sound almost like a formula, support is essential for a woman—or for anyone—tending to an Aids patient. Your local hotline will know if there is a nearby group. If there isn't, consider starting your own. "You're not going to make it without counseling or a group. The isolation is too terrible," says Suzanne, whose daughter Michelle died from drug-contracted Aids at age twenty-four. Suzanne was able to find a support group consisting of women who were caring for Aids patients; it included sisters, mothers, and friends of patients, as well as one woman whose lover was dying. Suzanne's other daughter also went to the group, as did her mother on occasion. Her husband went to a group just for male friends and relatives of patients.

"It got so I just waited from week to week for that one night with the group," Suzanne recalls. "I would have gone every night if I could. You have to deal with a great deal of anger and denial and guilt at first. I felt guilty because with anything else that could have happened to my children, I would have said, 'I'll take their place.' But I could not honestly say that about Aids. I couldn't wish it on me instead. And you get angry because you think they're responsible for getting a fatal disease. And then you feel more guilty because you're mad.

"But groups are also important for practical advice. You meet other people who are in different places with the disease—just a little ahead of you—and you hear about experimental drugs. The others in the group help keep you from making mistakes. And it's a lot easier to absorb the medical information by talking. You're in such a panic that it's hard to read and retain information."

As Aids becomes better understood and accepted, more families will want to keep a patient home throughout much of the illness. Doctors at major hospitals in large cities widely discourage patients from traveling great distances to these hospitals if it means depriving themselves of family support. The better plan for patients whose families are willing and able to take care of them is to stay at home as long as possible and be treated as an outpatient. Most smaller hospitals can treat Aids patients, and doctors at the major centers are very generous about giving their colleagues needed advice over the telephone. Nonetheless, no one—whether a mother, lover, wife, relative, or friend—who feels entirely intimidated by the idea should even attempt to care for an Aids patient at home. "We've seen some situations where a relative or lover starts doing this and then has to stop," says Len Martelli, author of *When Someone You Know Has Aids: A Practical Guide.* "If you just can't do it any more, that's a legitimate decision. The first thing to realize is that it's a two-person project—it involves you and the person who has Aids. You aren't a nurse or a handmaid. You have to have time for yourself, or else you get angry."

When family or friends keep a patient at home, some instruction about basic nursing and what to expect is helpful. American Red Cross chapters in New York, San Francisco, Los Angeles, Boston, and other cities now offers a six-session course on caring for Aids patients. It addresses nursing techniques, nutrition, hygiene and sanitation, medication, and the psychological demands of dealing with this illness. Whether the patient is hospitalized or at home, friends or family may also have to see to important practical and legal matters. It is particularly important, for example, to be sure that all of the patient's insurance policies are kept up to date and paid on time.

Visiting, comforting, and helping hospitalized Aids patients involves the same considerations as visiting other very sick people, as well as some extra efforts. In an excellent pamphlet, the New York City Gay Men's Health Crisis advises telephoning before visiting, celebrating holidays with patients, and bringing cheerful and useful small gifts—even newspapers are often hard to obtain in a hospital. "Don't be hesitant to share your faith with him," the pamphlet advises. "Spirituality can be very important at times such as these." It is particularly important to Aids patients, who often feel so shunned, to be touched: hold their hand, soothe their brow, or give them a backrub.

For women patients, gifts like make-up, which is impossible to obtain in hospitals, and pretty nightgowns, blouses, and scarves are good choices, so that they can continue to dress as they would want, even as they lose weight. "They need the niceties," says Marge Fenn. And women always want most to see and touch their children. "The families don't understand that mothers really still need to hold and embrace a child," she adds. "This frequently makes the other family members, particularly a grandmother, very nervous. She is already losing her daughter and cannot bear the idea that a grandchild is near the disease. We just have to educate families as much as possible."

Family members often prefer not to tell their own friends when a relative has Aids; and with such unreasonable fear about the disease, not telling too many people may help maintain a calmer and more loving atmosphere. "I've been very selective about who I tell even now," says Suzanne. "For instance, I work with young children, and I think some of their parents would worry. As a parent myself, before I really knew about the disease, I don't know how I would have felt about, say, a young child of mine going to school with a child who has Aids. Anyway, it's often easier just to say your child has died of a terminal illness. Most people assume it's cancer.

"I live in two different worlds now. The amazing thing is that, after two years, I still see many of the women from the support group. All of them now do volunteer work with patients or are involved in Aids prevention, as I am myself. In the end, you don't turn away from it. You go on to help instead."

The Future of Aids

"We have been given a treasured opportunity. Never before, when a sexually transmitted disease entered the human community, have we so quickly found the tools—including a test—to prevent its spread."—Dr. Robert Redfield

Between 1983 and 1985 there was a startling transformation in the distribution of Aids cases in Haiti. In 1983, only 22 percent of that nation's cases were heterosexually acquired, while 71 percent remained in the same major risk groups seen in the United States: homosexuals, bisexuals, drug abusers, and recipients of infected blood products. But two years later 72 percent of the newly reported cases were men and women who had contracted the virus from heterosexual intercourse. The Haitian experience is much closer to the American experience than to the situation in Africa, where the distribution of cases among men and women has been almost equal since the epidemic was recognized. (There has never been much doubt about heterosexual transmission in Africa.) What the pattern in Haiti confirms is that the virus can start in other groups and then rapidly spread to heterosexuals. This should hardly be surprising; the history of sexually transmitted diseases shows that they infect sexually active people, regardless of orientation or drug use. But many Americans still have trouble believing it could happen in the United States. "Considerable data from both Haiti and Africa now suggest that heterosexual transmission is the predominant mode of spread of the virus," says Dr. Warren D. Johnson, Chief of the Division of International Medicine at Cornell University Medical College, who has led a team of doctors studying the pattern of cases in Haiti. "Certainly, we have enough evidence to educate people that this could also be a probable scenario in the United States. I would prefer to be guilty of educating unnecessarily than be guilty of letting people get infected."

What could happen here? In the spring of 1986 the CDC predicted that there would be some 270,000 diagnosed Aids patients by 1991 and that 8.8 percent of them would be heterosexual—probably a serious underestimation. For one thing, this prediction assumed that the proportion of women's cases would not increase greatly from the current 5.5 percent of all cases. But the results of the Armed Services testing now suggest that women could easily constitute 25 percent of the cases by 1991. Moreover, the majority of women being diagnosed will almost certainly be heterosexual-contact cases, with those infected through drug use or contaminated blood products accounting for a smaller proportion of the total female caseload than they do now. But whatever the source of the infection, as the pool of infected women increases, so does the pool of infected heterosexual men. The real possibility is that heterosexual infection will account for 15 to 20 percent of all cases by 1991.

What the data in Haiti clearly show is that by the time 20 percent of diagnosed cases are heterosexual, the infection underneath has already become thoroughly heterosexual. At the point that officials in Haiti documented the heterosexual epidemic, it was impossible to stop. The important difference today is that we have a much better understanding of the disease itself as well as a test that can predict its pattern of spread. But we must use this knowledge. If Americans keep waiting for "proof" that heterosexual transmission can become the predominant mode of spread, they too will have lost their chance to prevent it.

The containment of Aids is hardly a contest between risk groups, although it has often been publicly presented as such. The point is not to constantly compare which groups have more casualties but to proceed with prevention across the board. Heterosexuals are lagging so far behind in prevention efforts, as the dismal venereal disease figures for 1986 show, that it is imperative they immediately understand the strategies available.

Experience with the original risk groups suggests that, even with a late start, amazing inroads in prevention can be made rapidly. For example, as the lesson of not sharing needles has taken hold, infection among drug addicts in northern California has held steady at about 10 percent for the past year. In Minnesota, which has made intense efforts to educate homosexuals and has strongly encouraged them to be tested, the infection rate for homosexuals rose only from 14 percent to 15 percent in the past year, a remarkable record at that level of infection. It means that *almost nobody,* or at least almost nobody who is sufficiently educated to seek testing and continued counseling, is being sexually irresponsible.

Heterosexual hemophiliacs and male drug addicts who are well educated about Aids are generally very careful not to spread the virus; in both groups, education has been backed by wide testing. While many observers have been astonished to see such a similar sense of responsibility in such different groups—one predominantly white and middle-class, the other mostly low-income and black or Hispanic—what we are really seeing is nothing more than a fundamental human response. Most men, once they understand that they could transmit HIV, want to protect their wives and loved ones from a fatal disease. It is that simple.

The challenge is to reach the legion of heterosexuals who do not yet feel the close threat of Aids. Breaking through denial—"It can't happen to me, so it isn't happening here"—has repeatedly been the first task in controlling epidemics. What fools so many Americans and Europeans is that media saturation has made them think they understand Aids far better than they do. Yet they do not understand how deceptive "case counts" are as a standard for judging the epidemic; nor can they grasp the implications of government and media projections that, by focusing on cases rather than infection, are necessarily five years out of date. For women, as we have seen, the risk-group and case-count way of looking at Aids is particularly dangerous. It has given them the impression that they are insulated from the disease—when they are not.

For actual Aids prevention, you have to go much further. You have to dismiss the endless reports about risk groups and learn about the possible risks of your own behavior. You have to surmount fear and accept responsibility. No matter how tired you get of hearing about Aids, you have to stay alert and educate yourself about what Aids has to do with you and yours.

If news reports are not education, then what is? A pamphlet about Aids in your hand—whoever you are—that says Aids is a problem for you. A televised public-service announcement about condoms that is addressed to your gender, your sexual orientation, and your ethnic group. Lectures about Aids in your union hall, your office, your gym, your professional society, or your women's club—with specific answers to questions that have been bothering you. By these basic standards, there is still almost no Aids education anywhere in the world.

If we do choose to educate and inspire we don't have to ask if it will work. It will. But we have precious little time, and we must move fast. Above all, let us not pretend that we lack the knowledge. And let us not complain that Aids prevention means the end of love.

Guarding life is not the end of love; it is the beginning.

Looking at Your Own Risks

This questionnaire is meant for you to answer privately, to help you assess your risk of having been exposed to HIV. It can neither diagnose Aids nor tell you whether you have contracted HIV. Its purpose is to make you aware of the potential risks of your overall behavior.

While this questionnaire is meant for women, you might well want to share it with your partner so that he, too, can look more closely at his possible risks. (If it is used by a man, a question about bisexuality must be added: Has he had unprotected anal intercourse with another man in the past five years? A "yes" answer adds 20 points to the score.)

Each answer has a point value, shown at the left in parentheses. Remember, a high total score does not mean you have contracted HIV—nor does a low score guarantee you haven't. You should ask a doctor or health counselor about any specific worries you may have after assessing your risk.

1. In the past ten years I have had
   (1) _____ one sex partner
   (2) _____ 2–4 partners

(3) _____ 5–9 partners
(6) _____ 10 or more partners

2. Most of my sexual contacts during the past three years were in (check up to two answers that most apply to you):
   (1) _____ a steady relationship or marriage that I believe is monogamous
   (3) _____ a relationship in which I have been monogamous but my partner may not have been
   (5) _____ multiple relationships with partners pretty well known to me
   (10) _____ multiple relationships with partners I don't know well

3. My sexual activities during the past three years include (check all that apply to you):
   (4) _____ unprotected (no condom) vaginal or anal intercourse with a partner whose Aids risks I have not discussed
   (3) _____ vaginal or anal intercourse using condoms
   (2) _____ unprotected vaginal or anal intercourse in a long-term monogamous relationship
   (1) _____ oral sex
   (0) _____ kissing, massage, masturbation

4. The following best describes my discussions about Aids with my present partner or partners during the past three years (check the one that most applies to you today):
   (25) _____ I know my partner has an Aids risk—we've discussed that—but we still haven't gone for counseling or testing
   (20) _____ I suspect a partner has a risk for Aids, but we haven't discussed it
   (4) _____ I've discussed Aids with my current partner

and there are no evident risks, but I haven't looked into the past

(1) _____ I have discussed Aids with my current and past partners; I am not aware of any risks

5. The following best describes my drug use (check one):
(25) _____ I have injected drugs in the past five years
(20) _____ I gave up injecting drugs six to ten years ago
(6) _____ my use of alcohol or noninjected drugs (cocaine, amyl or butyl nitrite, marijuana, Quaaludes, amphetamines, or other substances) sometimes leads me to have sexual encounters I'd like to forget about

6. The following best describes my current attitude toward Aids (check one):
(4) _____ I really don't think I could ever get it
(3) _____ I believe anyone can get it from sex or injecting drugs, but I still don't want to think about it
(2) _____ I am obsessed with Aids but still reluctant to discuss it with anyone
(1) _____ I am trying to learn about risk behaviors and discuss the subject with male and female friends

7. Most of my sexual encounters during the past five years were in (check one):
(3) _____ the New York metropolitan area; northern New Jersey; Wilmington, Baltimore, Washington, D.C., Chicago, Las Vegas, and surrounding areas; San Francisco and nearby counties; greater Los Angeles; Houston-Dallas; southern Florida; Puerto Rico

(2) _____ other large urban areas (Boston, Atlanta, Seattle, Philadelphia, etc.)

(1) _____ small towns, rural areas, central farm states

8. My race or ethnic group is:

(3) _____ black or Hispanic

(2) _____ white

(1) _____ oriental, other

9. My age is:

(2) _____ under 35

(1) _____ 35 or older

To determine your score, add up the numbers beside each answer checked.

My score is _____ .

KEY:

32 or more: High risk. You should talk to a counselor to learn more about your risk behaviors and consider getting an HIV test.

25 to 31: Medium risk. You should consider counseling and getting an HIV test.

21 to 24: Moderate risk. You should consider any changes that could lower your risk even further.

20 or less: Low risk. You should continue to monitor your risks carefully and make sure your partner understands the Aids risk behaviors.

(Partly based on a scoring system suggested by the American College Health Association and used in consultation with the association.)

A p p e n d i x

Male-to-Female HIV Transmission

Type of Study Population	Rate of Female HIV Infection (percent)	Study
Wives of recently diagnosed patients	44	Montefiore Medical Center, Bronx, New York
Wives of recently diagnosed patients	42	Miami Aids Clinical Research Unit
Previously uninfected wives of diagnosed patients after a year of sexual intercourse using condoms	12	"
Previously uninfected wives of diagnosed patients after a year of sexual intercourse without condoms	86	"

Type of Study Population	Rate of Female HIV Infection (percent)	Study
Women who had stopped dating or living with a man months or years prior to his Aids diagnosis	19	San Francisco Department of Health Contact Tracing Program
Wives and girlfriends of mixed groups of asymptomatic HIV carriers and diagnosed patients who were:		Berkeley Partner Study, University of California at Berkeley
hemophiliacs	10	
transfusion recipients	15	
bisexuals	19	
drug abusers	46	
Female partners of infected sailor ("Lars")	57	Sweden

The Ten Leading Places for Aids

As the epidemic spreads to younger populations, new areas are more severely affected.

Diagnosed Aids cases as percent of all American cases		Rate of HIV infection among young armed-forces recruits of both sexes	
Place	**percent**	**Place**	**rate per 1,000**
1. New York	32.0	1. Washington, D.C.	10.0
2. California	24.0	2. Puerto Rico	9.0
3. Florida	6.0	3. New York	4.0
4. New Jersey	6.0	4. Maryland	4.0
5. Texas	5.5	5. New Jersey	3.5
6. Illinois	2.0	6. Nevada	3.5
7. Pennsylvania	2.0	7. Delaware	2.0
8. Massachusetts	2.0	8. California	2.0
9. Georgia	2.0	9. Florida	2.0
10. Washington, D.C.	2.0	10. Texas	2.0

Aids Hotlines

National Hotline: Centers for Disease Control 800-447-AIDS

Alabama
Birmingham | Birmingham Aids Outreach | 205-930-0440

California
Costa Mesa | Aids Response Team | 714-534-0862
Fresno | Central Valley Aids Team | 209-264-2437
Los Angeles | Aids Project | 800-922-2437 (in California)
| Los Angeles Lesbian & Gay Community Services Center | 213-464-7400
San Diego | San Diego Aids Project | 619-543-0300
San Francisco | San Francisco Aids Foundation | 415-853-2437
San Rafael | Marin Aids Support Network | 415-457-2437

Colorado
Denver | Colorado Aids Project | 303-837-0166

Connecticut

Hartford	Aids Project, Hartford	203-247-2437
New Haven	Aids Project, New Haven	203-624-2437

Delaware

Wilmington	State Aids Program Office	800-422-0429 (in Delaware)
	Delaware Lesbian/Gay Health Advocates	same

District of Columbia

Washington	Aids Education Fund	202-332-5939

Florida

Fort Lauderdale	Aids Center One	800-325-5371
Miami	Health Crisis Network	305-634-4636
West Palm Beach	INFORUM	305-582-4357

Illinois

Chicago	Howard Brown Memorial Clinic	312-871-5696
	Aids Action Project	800-AID-AIDS (in Illinois)

Iowa

Des Moines	Aids Project of Central Iowa Red Cross	800-445-2437 (in Iowa)

Maryland

Baltimore	Health Education and Resources Organization (HERO)	301-685-1180

Massachusetts

Boston	Aids Action Committee	800-235-2331 (in Massachusetts)

Nevada

Las Vegas	Aid for Aids of Nevada	702-369-6163

New Mexico

Santa Fe	New Mexico Aids Services	800-858-2437

New York

Albany	Aids Council of Northeastern New York	518-445-2437
Buffalo	Western New York Aids Project	716-847-2437
New York	Department of Health	718-HTLV-111
	Gay Men's Health Crisis	212-807-6655
Rochester	Aids Rochester	716-232-4430
Huntington Station	Long Island Association for Aids Care	516-385-2437
Syracuse	Central New York Aids Task Force	315-475-2437

Ohio

| Cleveland | Health Issues Task Force | 216-651-1448 |
| Columbus | Columbus Aids Task Force | 614-224-0411 |

Pennsylvania

| Philadelphia | Philadelphia Aids Task Force | 215-732-2437 |

Tennessee

| Nashville | Nashville CARES | 615-321-0118 |

Texas

Austin	Austin Aids Project	512-452-9550
Dallas	Aids Resource Center	214-521-5124
Houston	Aids Foundation	715-524-2437

Utah

| Salt Lake City | Aids Project Utah | 801-486-2437 |

Wisconsin

| Milwaukee | Milwaukee Aids Project | 800-334-2437 |

Organizations

For Women

San Francisco Aids Foundation*
Women's Program
Nancy Shaw, Coordinator
333 Valencia Street
San Francisco, California 94103
415-864-4376

AWARE
Ward 84
San Francisco General Hospital
995 Potrero Avenue
San Francisco, California 94110
415-476-4091
   Education and research

*denotes women's support group available

Stuyvesant Polyclinic*
Women and Aids Counseling Group
137 Second Avenue
New York, New York 10003
212-674-0267
  Contact: Dooley Worth

Minority Task Force on Aids of the Council of Churches of
  the City of New York*
Suki Ports, Director
92 St. Nicholas Avenue
New York, New York 10026
212-749-2816

Aids Action Committee*
Women at Risk Group
661 Boylston Street
Boston, Massachusetts 02116
617-437-6200
  Contact: Pat Giulino

Gay and Lesbian Counseling Services Alternative Test Site*
6 Hamilton Place
Boston, Massachusetts 02108
617-542-5188
  Contact: Clay

The Women's Aids Project*
8235 Santa Monica Boulevard
West Hollywood, California 90046
213-650-1508

Women and Aids Project
1209 Decater Street, NW
Washington, D.C. 20011

---

*denotes women's support group available

For Parents

Mothers of Aids Patients Counseling hotlines:
Betty Clare Moffitt
213-450-6485 (Santa Monica, California)
Barbara Cleaver
213-530-2109 (Lomita, California)
Mary Jane Edwards
213-541-3134 (Redondo, California)
 Materials:
 When Someone You Love Has AIDS
 by Betty Clare Moffitt
 Available for $9.95 from
 I.B.S. Press
 2339 28th Street
 Santa Monica, California 90405
 213-450-6485

Gay Men's Health Crisis
254 West 18th Street
New York, New York 10011
212-807-6655
 Support groups for parents

San Francisco Aids Foundation
333 Valencia Street
San Francisco, California 94103
415-864-4376
 Support groups for parents

For Drug Abusers

ADAPT
163 Joralemon Street
Brooklyn, New York 11201
212-807-5560
 Newsletter and brochures available

Pregnancy and Addiction Program
Boston City Hospital
818 Harrison Avenue
Boston, Massachusetts 02118
617-424-5094

Treatment Alternatives to Street Crimes
1500 N. Halsted Street
Chicago, Illinois 60622
312-787-0208

Haight Ashbury Free Medical Clinic
529 Clayton Street
San Francisco, California 94117
415-431-2450

For Hemophiliacs

World Hemophilia Aids Center
2400 S. Flower Street
Los Angeles, California 90007
213-742-1357
  Materials:
  Hemophilia World, quarterly newsletter on
  hemophilia and international Aids research
  (free)

National Hemophilia Foundation
Resource and Consultation Center for Aids/HIV Infection
Peggy Heine, M.S.W., Director
110 Greene Street
New York, New York 10012
212-219-8180

For Students

American College Health Association
Task Force on Aids
15879 Crabbs Branch Way
Rockville, Maryland 20855
301-963-1100
  Materials:
  The AIDS Dilemma: Higher Education's Response (video)
  AIDS on the College Campus (special report)
  AIDS—What Everyone Should Know (pamphlet)

Atlanta University Core Aids Education Committee
Rudolph E. Jackson, M.D., Chairman
Morehouse School of Medicine
720 Westview Drive SW
Atlanta, Georgia 30310
404-752-1500
  Developing materials for black colleges and other colleges

For Haitians

Haitian Coalition
Marie St. Cyr, Director
50 Court Street
Brooklyn, New York 11201
718-855-0972
  Education and counseling

For Hispanics

Hispanic Aids Forum
853 Broadway
New York, New York 10003
212-673-7320

For People with Aids (PWA)

National Association of People with Aids
1012 14th Street, NW
Washington, D.C. 20005
202-347-1317
  Materials:
  Hints for the Newly Diagnosed
  A book of essays by Aids patients
  Free to people with Aids; $5 for others

People with Aids Coalition
263A West 19th Street
New York, New York 10011
212-627-1810
  Materials:
  PWA Coalition Newsline
  A monthly newsletter free to people
  with Aids and $20 annually for others

National Educational Campaigns

American Red Cross
National Headquarters
17th and D Streets, NW
Washington, D.C. 20006
202-639-3220
  Materials include:
  Beyond Fear (three-part video)
  Pamphlets on every aspect of Aids
  Check local chapters for availability of
  home-nursing course for those taking care
  of Aids patients

Southern Christian Leadership Conference
Aids Project
334 Auburn Avenue, NE
Atlanta, Georgia, 30303
404-522-1420
  Pamphlets and videos on
  Aids and the black community

Books and Educational Materials

Please be fair! When sending for pamphlets (except to government agencies) always include $1.00 and a stamped, self-addressed envelope. The nonprofit Aids-education organizations usually have small budgets, and a larger donation is always appreciated.

For Women

Women Address AIDS
(Includes safer-sex guidelines.)
Women's Aids Project
8235 Santa Monica Boulevard
West Hollywood, California 90046

Women Need to Know about AIDS
(Includes safer-sex guidelines.)
Gay Men's Health Crisis
254 West 18th Street
New York, New York 10011

Lesbians and AIDS
Women's Aids Network
333 Valencia Street
San Francisco, California 94103

AIDS and Safer Sex for Women
(Guidelines for bisexual and lesbian women.)
Fenway Community Health Center
16 Haviland Street
Boston, Massachusetts 02115

Women and AIDS Clinical Resource Guide
(Massive and detailed guidance for setting up clinical programs for
    women.)
San Francisco Aids Foundation
333 Valencia Street
San Francisco, California 94103
    Cost is $40 plus $3 for shipping.

General

AIDS and the Black Community
Southern Christian Leadership Conference Aids Project
334 Auburn Avenue, NE
Atlanta, Georgia 30303

How to Talk to Your Children about AIDS
SIECUS
32 Washington Place
New York, New York 10003

What Everyone Should Know about AIDS
(Nongraphic pamphlet with cartoonlike characters explaining how Aids
    is and is not spread. Good for pre-adolescents.)
U.S. Public Health Service
Aids Clearing House
P.O. Box 14252
Washington, D.C. 20004

Straight Talk about Sex and AIDS
(Encourages men and women to talk about their sexual and drug histories and to discuss and take sexual precautions. Available in Spanish.)
San Francisco Aids Foundation
333 Valencia Street
San Francisco, California 94103

When a Friend Has AIDS
(Guidance for friends and family.)
Gay Men's Health Crisis
254 West 18th Street
New York, New York 10011

La Comunidád y SIDA and
Informaciónes médicas sobre SIDA
Hispanic Aids Forum
853 Broadway, 5th floor
New York, New York 10003

You Don't Have to Be White or Gay to Get AIDS
(Striking pamphlet on prenatal transmission.)
HERO
101 West Read Street
Baltimore, Maryland 21201

R e f e r e n c e s

Because Aids information is being disseminated so quickly it is difficult to footnote in a standard fashion. Much Aids information has been presented at meetings and seminars. Since few people have access to the programs or abstracts from such meetings, I have limited these references to the major published studies relevant to each chapter. Large parts of this book are also based on interviews or personal communications. Those sources are obvious within the text and I have cited personal communications only from overseas.

Introduction: Women and Aids

Burke, D.F., Brundage, J.F., and Bernier, W., "Demography of HIV Infections Among Military Recruit Applicants in New York City," *New York State Journal of Medicine,* 1987.

Clumet, N., et al., "Heterosexual Promiscuity Among African Patients with AIDS," *New England Journal of Medicine,* July 18, 1985, p. 182.

Chapter One: The Virus at Work

Chamberland, M.E., et al., "Acquired Immunodeficiency in the United States: An Analysis of Cases Outside High-Incidence Groups," *Annals of Internal Medicine* 101 (1984), pp. 617–23.

"Classification System for Human T-Lymphotropic Virus Type III/Lymphadenopathy-Associated Virus Infections," MMWR, May 23, 1986, pp. 334–39.

Fischl, M., et al., "Evaluation of Heterosexual Partners, Children and Household Contacts of Adults with Aids," *Journal of the American Medical Association* 257 (1987), pp. 640–44.

Franzén, C., National Bacteriological Laboratory, Stockholm, Sweden. "Chain of Heterosexual Transmission of HIV," presentation at the International Conference on Aids, Paris, June, 1986, and personal communication.

Kingsley, L.A., et al., "Risk Factors for Seroconversion to HIV Among Male Homosexuals," *Lancet*, Feb. 14, 1987, pp. 345–48.

McCray, E., and the Cooperative Needlestick Surveillance Group, "Occupational Risk of the Acquired Immune Deficiency Syndrome Among Health Care Workers," *New England Journal of Medicine* 314 (1986) pp. 1127–32.

"New AIDS Studies Focus on Its Spread," AP in *The New York Times*, Oct. 1, 1986, p. B6.

Winkelstein et al., "Sexual Practices and Risk of Infection by HIV," *Journal of the American Medical Association* 257 (1987), pp. 321–25.

Chapter Two: Which Men Have Aids?

"AIDS and Intravenous Drug Abusers," *British Journal of Addiction* 81 (1986), pp. 307–10.

Bakeman, R., et al., "AIDS Risk-Group Profiles in Whites and Members of Minority Groups," *New England Journal of Medicine,* July 17, 1986, p. 191.

Brunet, J.B., et al., "AIDS Surveillance in Europe," *Revue d'Épidémiologie et de Santé Publique* 34 (1986), pp. 126–33.

Centers for Disease Control, "Acquired Immunodeficiency Syndrome—Weekly AIDS Surveillance," March 16, 1987.

Jason, J., et al., "HTLV-III Antibody: Association with Blood-Component Usage," *Journal of the American Medical Association* 253 (1985), pp. 3409–15.

Norman, C., "Military AIDS Testing Offers Research Bonus," *Science,* May 16, 1986, p. 818.

Tauris, P., "Heterosexuals Importing HIV from Africa," *Lancet,* Feb. 7, 1987, p. 325.

Chapter Three: Personal Prevention

Fischl et al., "Evaluation" (cited in Chapter 1).

Marmor, M., et al., "Possible Female-to-Female Transmission of Human Immunodeficiency Virus," *Annals of Internal Medicine* 105 (1986), p. 969.

Chapter Four: Public Imperatives

Bayer, R., Levine, C., and Wolf, S., "HIV Antibody Screening: An Ethical Framework for Evaluating Proposed Programs," *Journal of the American Medical Association* 256 (1986), pp. 1768–74.

Des Jarlais, D.C., et al., "Heterosexual Partners: A Large Risk Group for AIDS," *Lancet,* Dec. 8, 1984, pp. 1346–47.

Chapter Five: Drugs, Prostitution, and the Heterosexual Connection

Friedman, S.R., Des Jarlais, D.C., Sotheran, J.L., "AIDS Health Education for Intravenous Drug Users," *Health Education Quarterly,* Fall-Winter, 1986.

Smith, G. L. and Smith, K. F., "Lack of HIV Infection and Condom Use in Licensed Prostitutes," *Lancet,* Dec. 13, 1986, p. 1392.

Chapter Six: Blood

Cordell, R.R., et al., "Experience with 11,916 Designated Donors," *Transfusion* 26 (1986), pp. 484–86.

Kuritsky, J. N., Schorr, J.B., et al., "Results of Nationwide Screening of Blood and Plasma for Antibodies to Human T-Cell Lymphotrophic Virus, Type III," *Transfusion* 26 (1986), pp. 205–7.

Chapter Seven: What'll We Tell the Kids?

Koop, C. E., *Surgeon General's Report on Acquired Immune Deficiency Syndrome,* (Washington, D.C.: U.S. Public Health Service, November, 1986).

Afterword: The Future of Aids

Altman, L.K., "A Striking Shift Is Seen in Haiti in AIDS Victims," *New York Times,* June 29, 1986, p. 1.

Index

About the Author

Christopher Norwood, writer and medical journalist, is a graduate of Wellesley College. Her first book, *About Paterson: The Making and Unmaking of an American City,* was chosen by the *New York Times* as a "Significant Book of the Year" and her second, *At Highest Risk: The Effects of Environmental Hazards on the Fetus and Child,* was named an "Important Medical Science Book of the Year" by *Library Journal.* She has written for many major publications, including *Ms., New York,* and *Mother Jones,* and her articles on Aids have appeared in *Mademoiselle, Us,* the *Village Voice,* and *Newsday.*

Ms. Norwood is a former communications director of the New York City Health and Hospitals Corporation. She is currently chair of the Aids Committee of the New York City chapter of the National Women's Health Network.